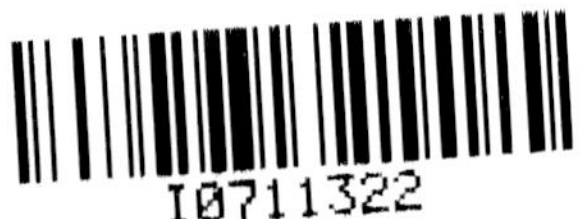

Mandala Coloring Book

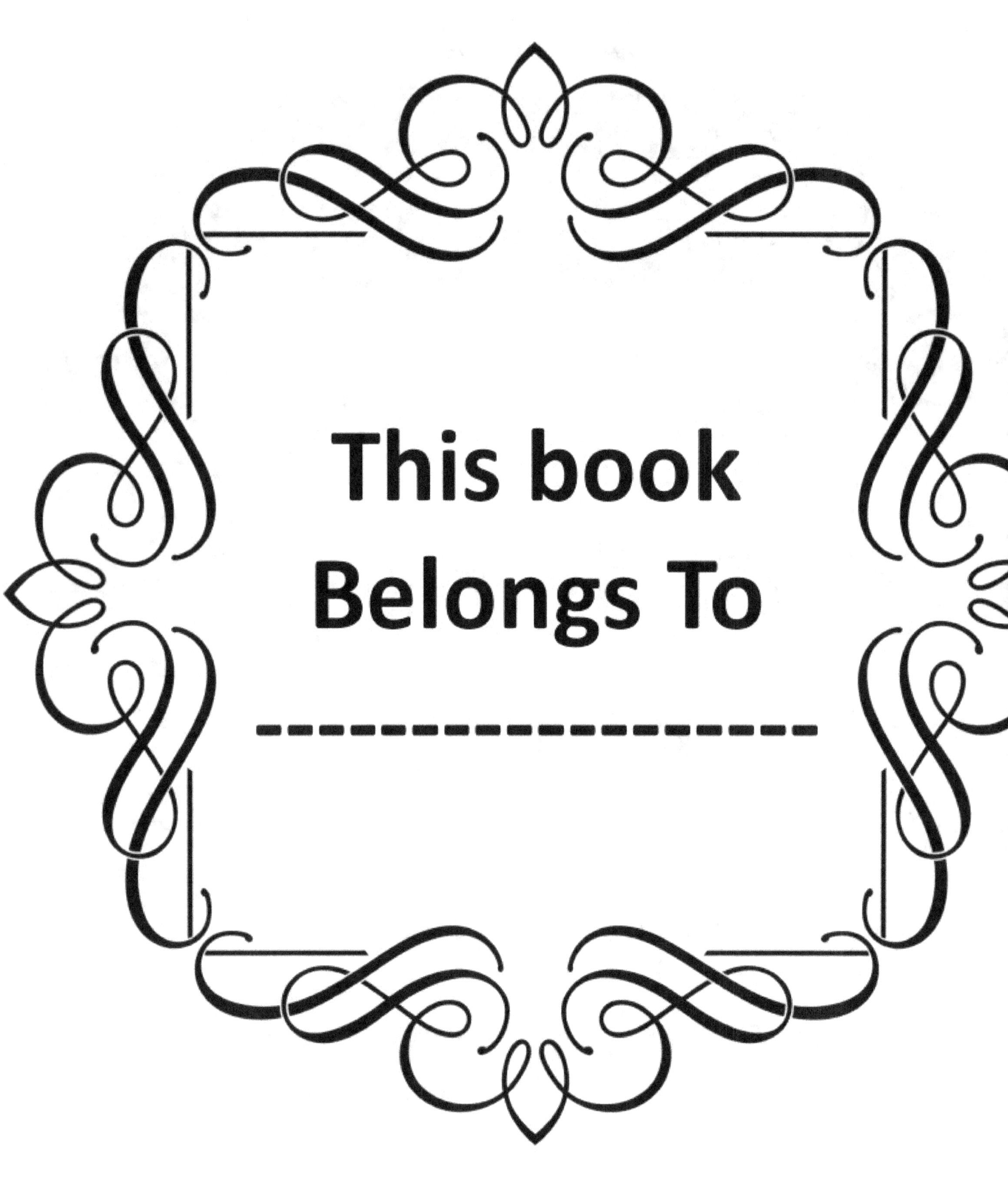
This book
Belongs To
____

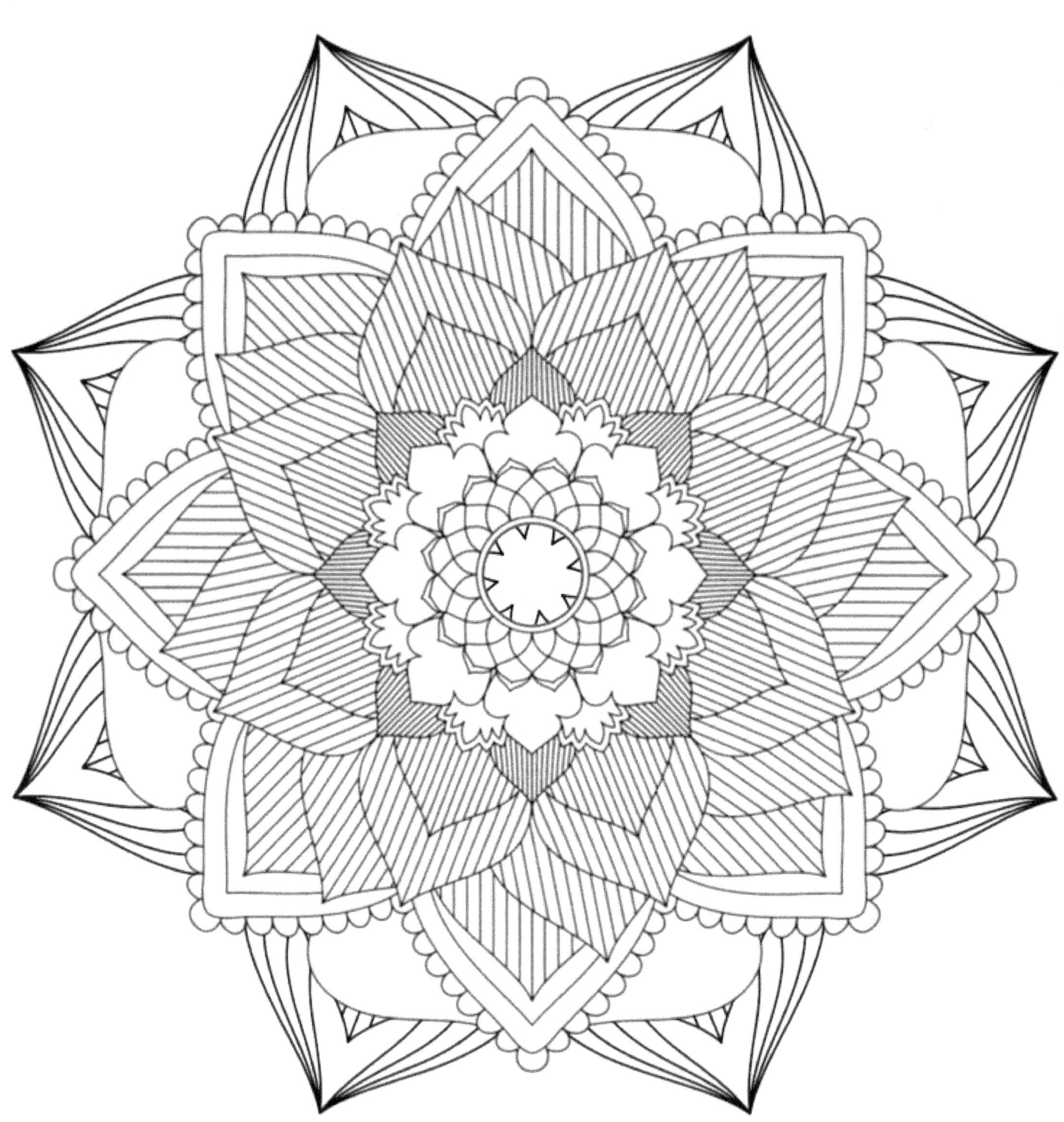

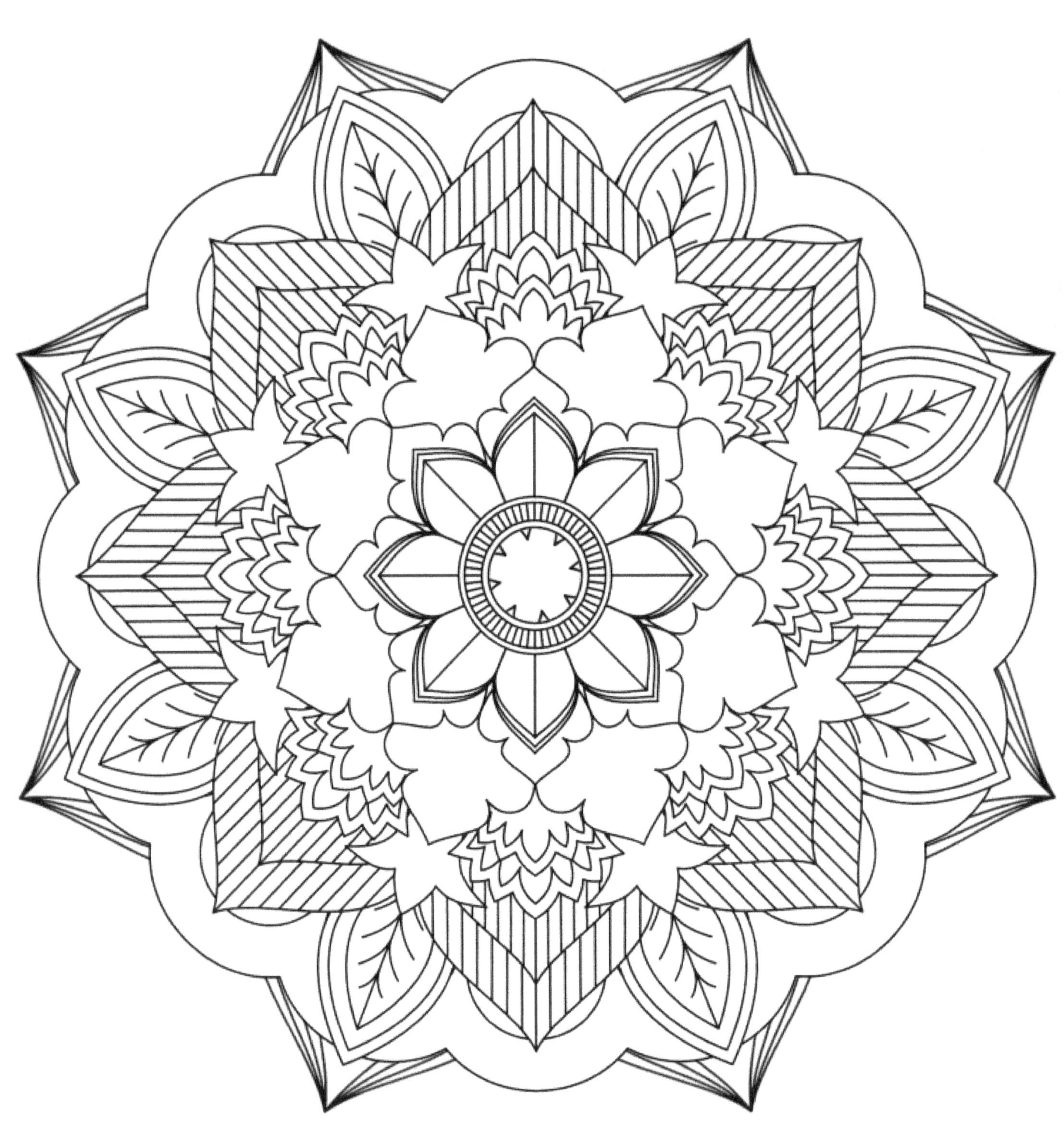

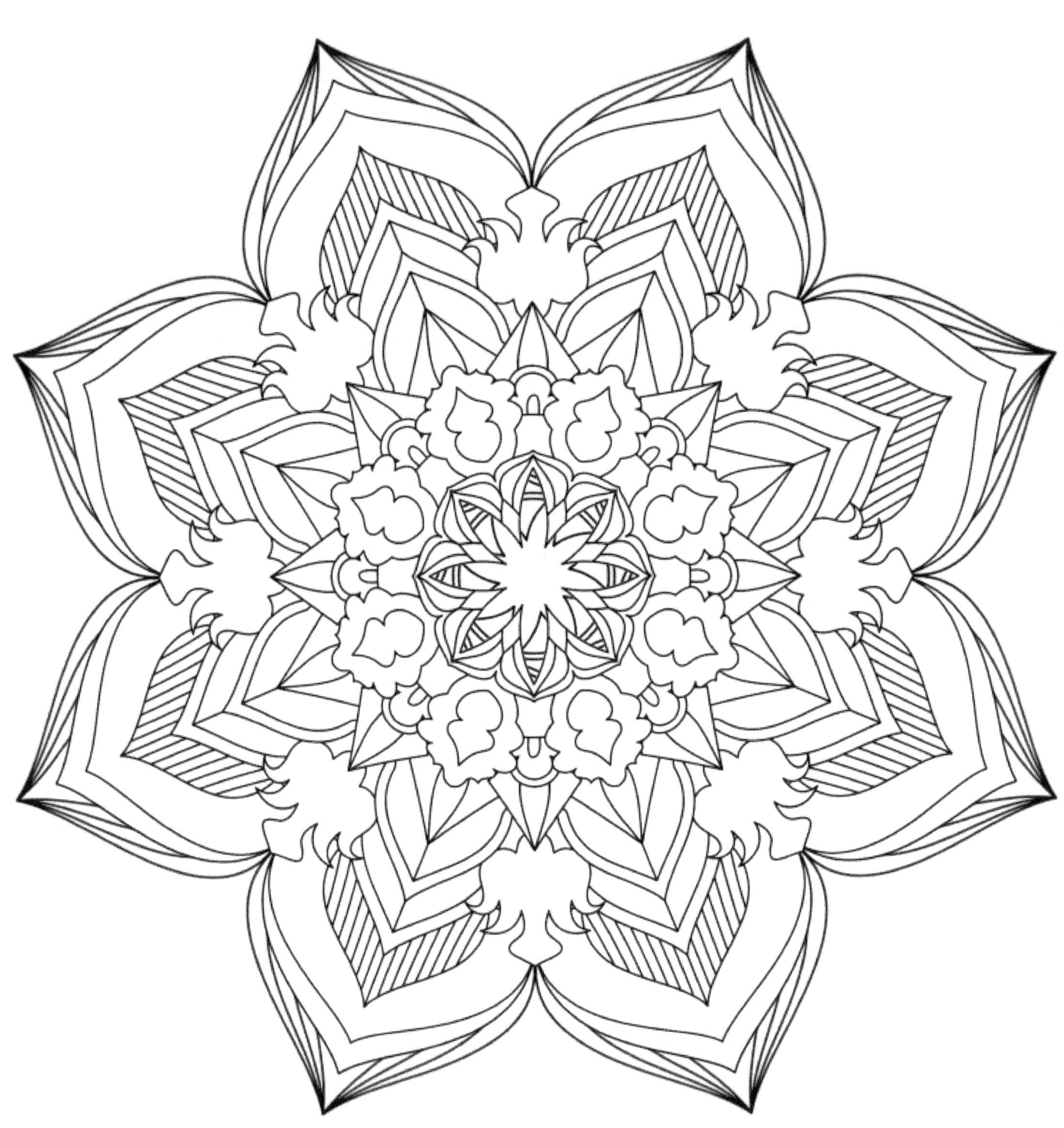

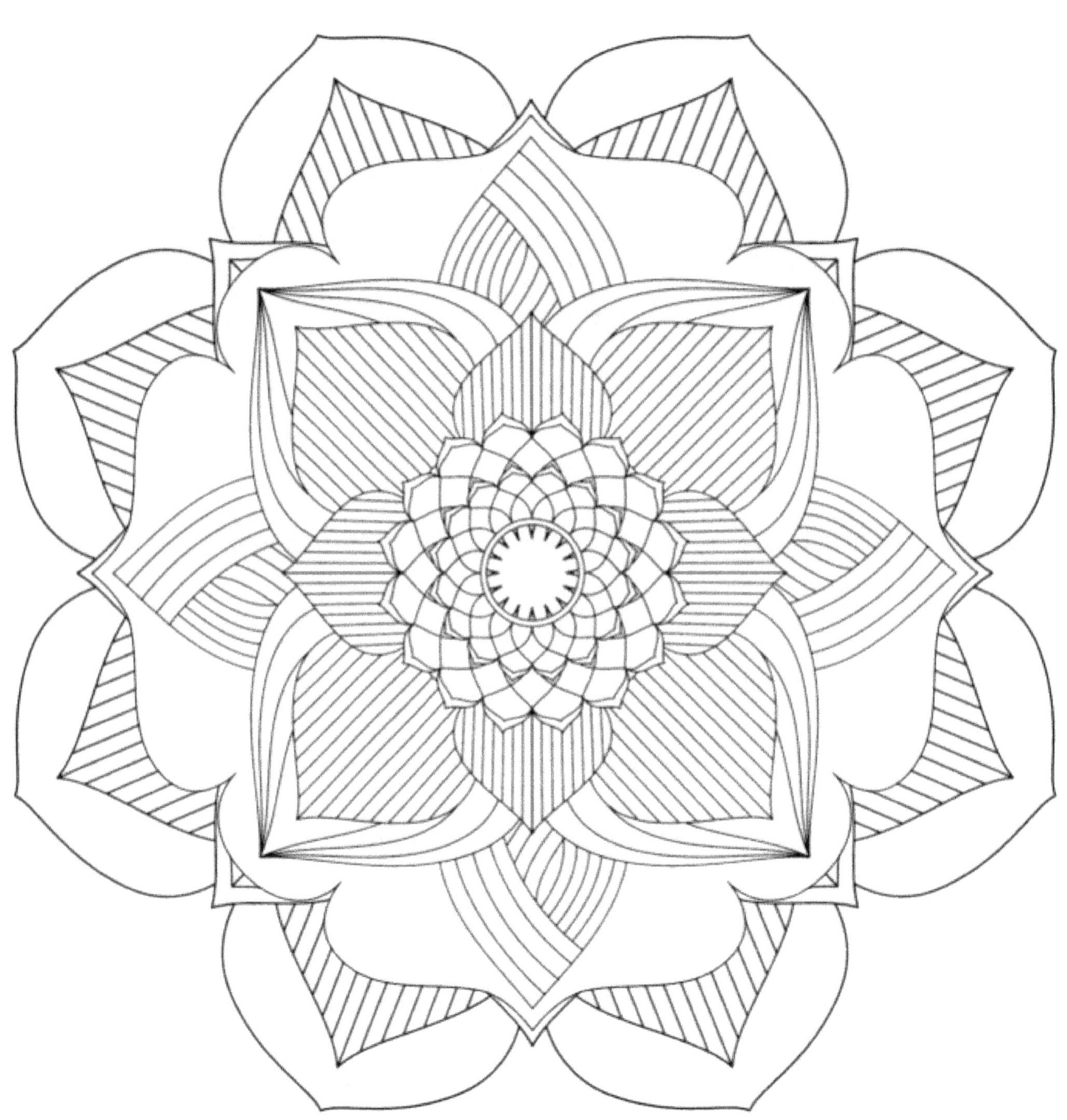

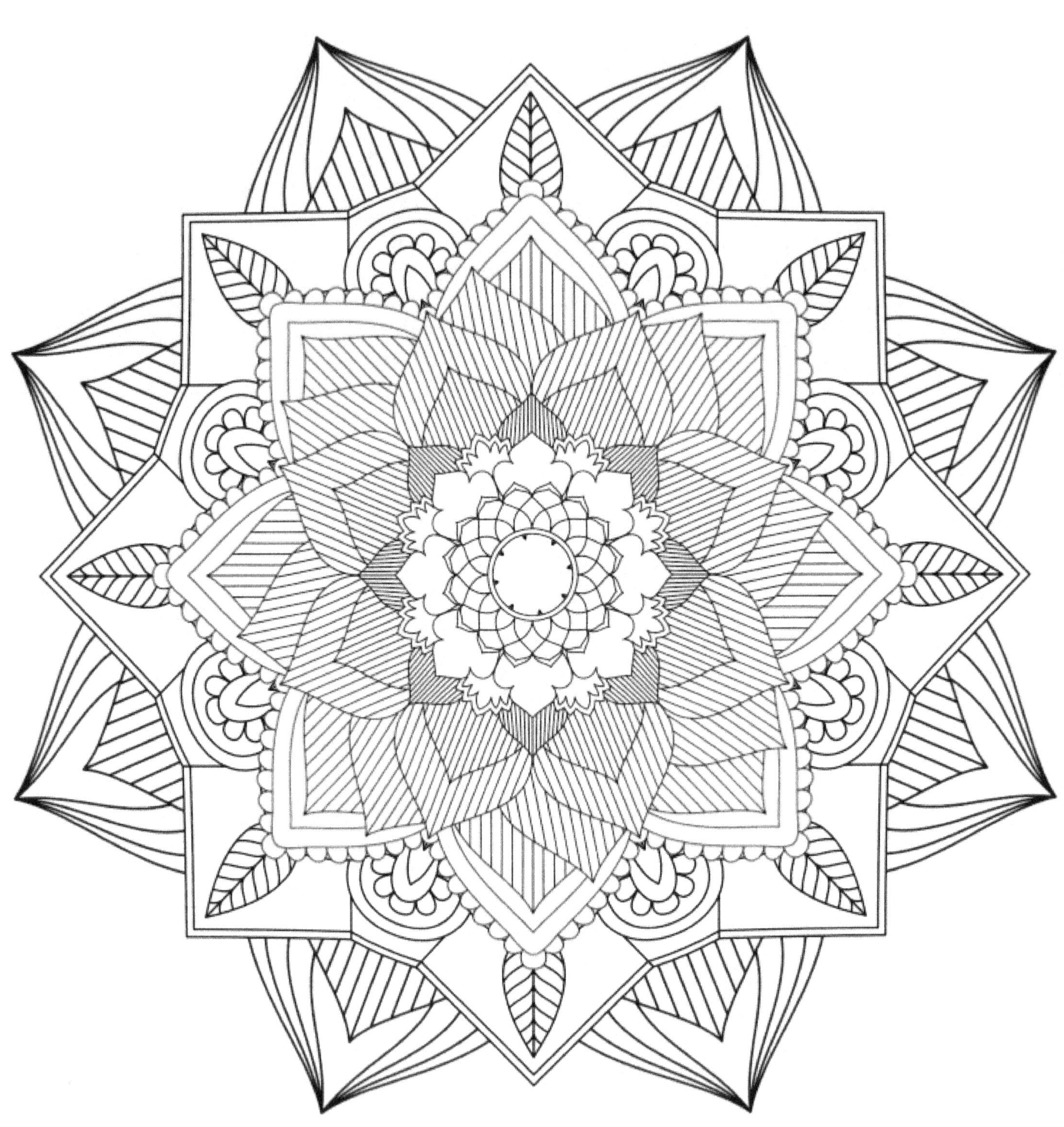

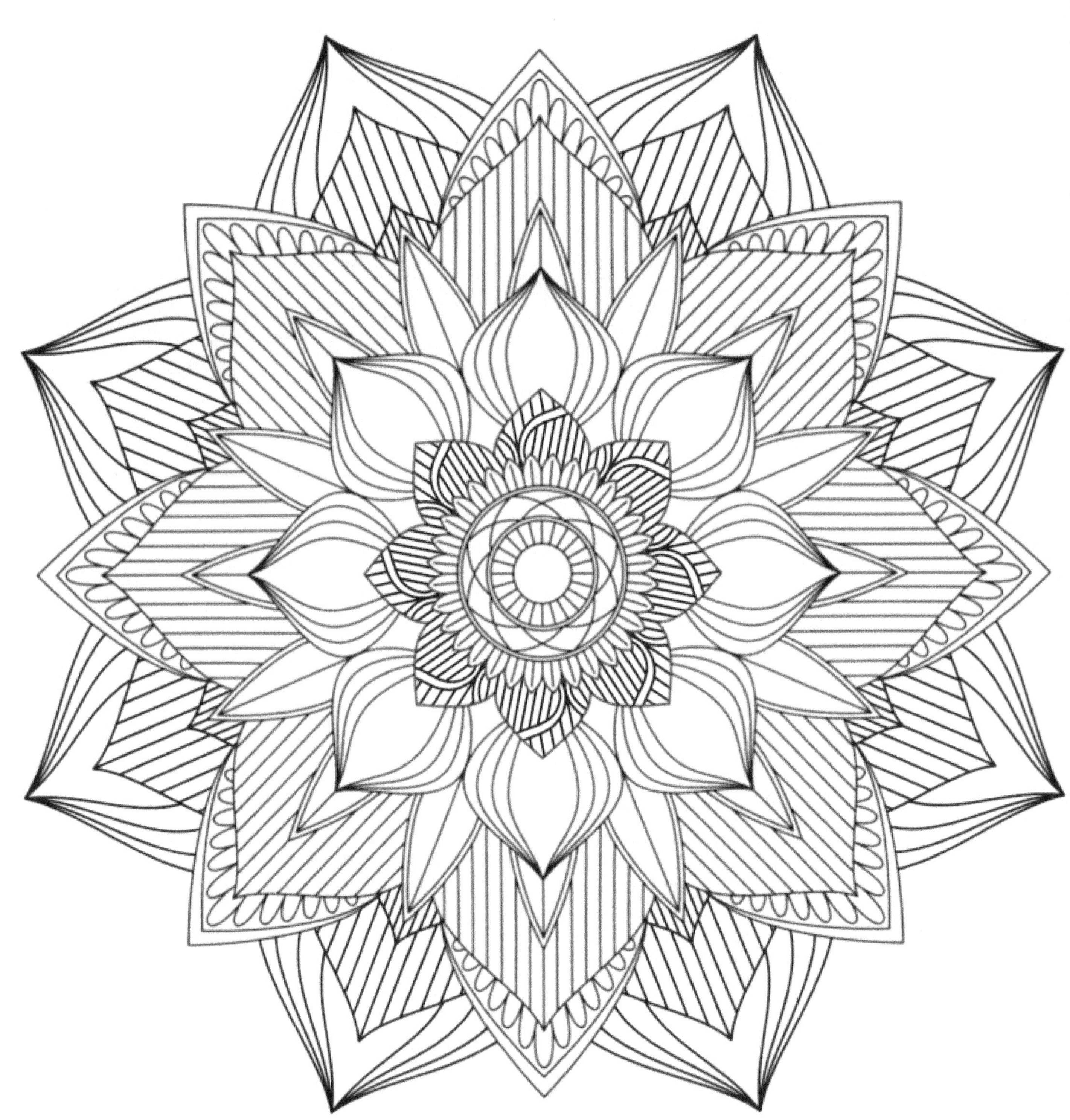

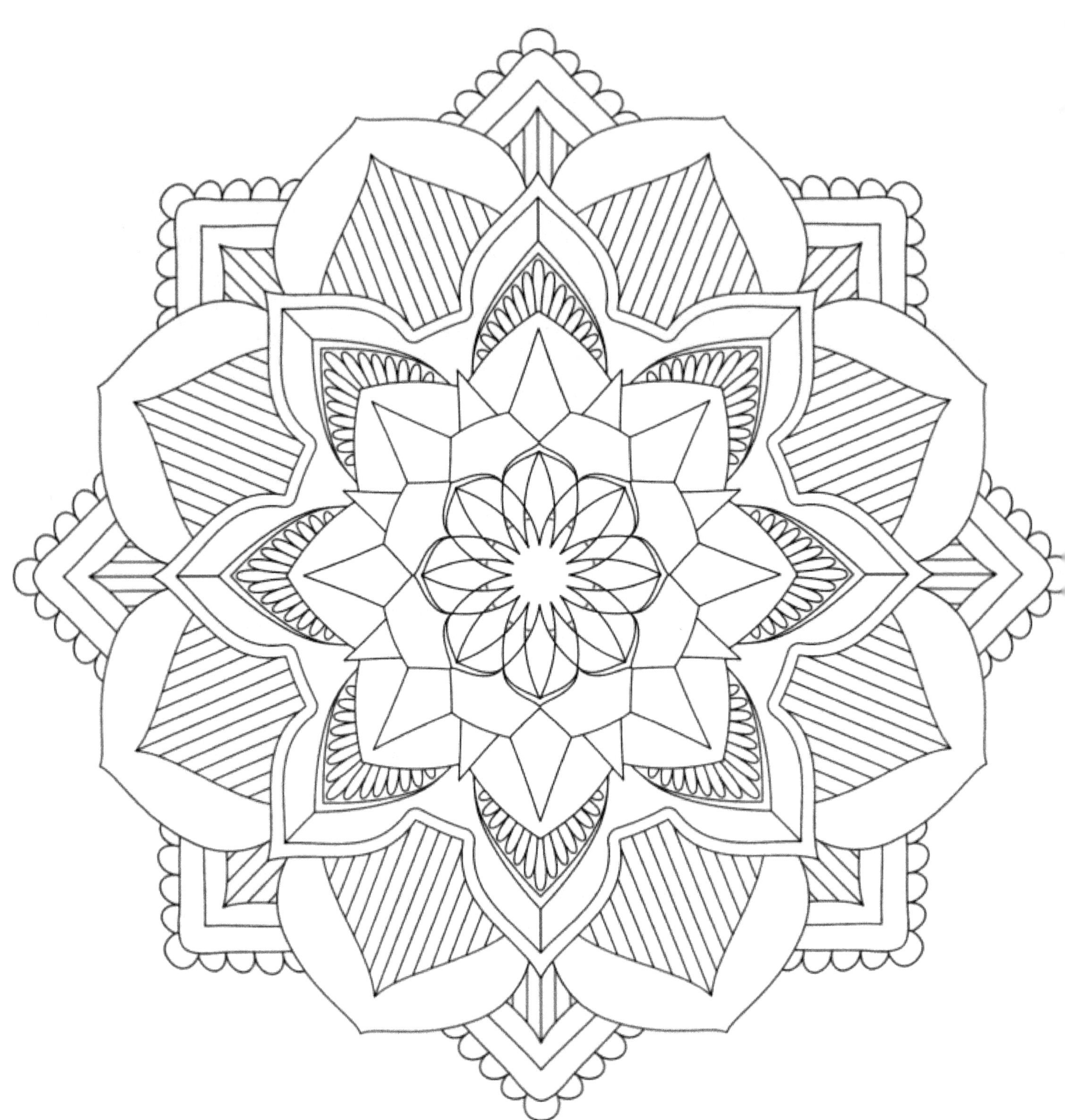

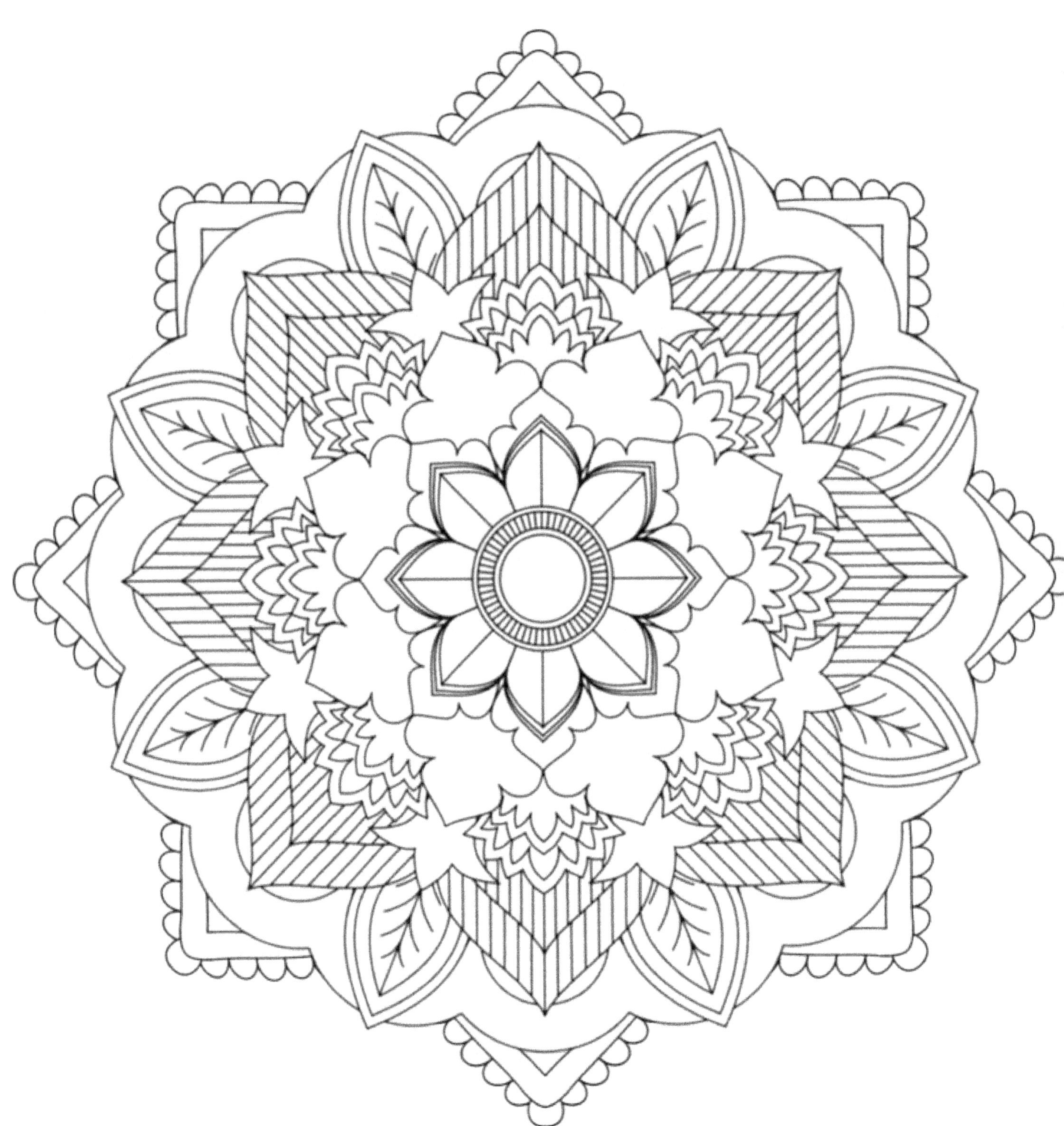

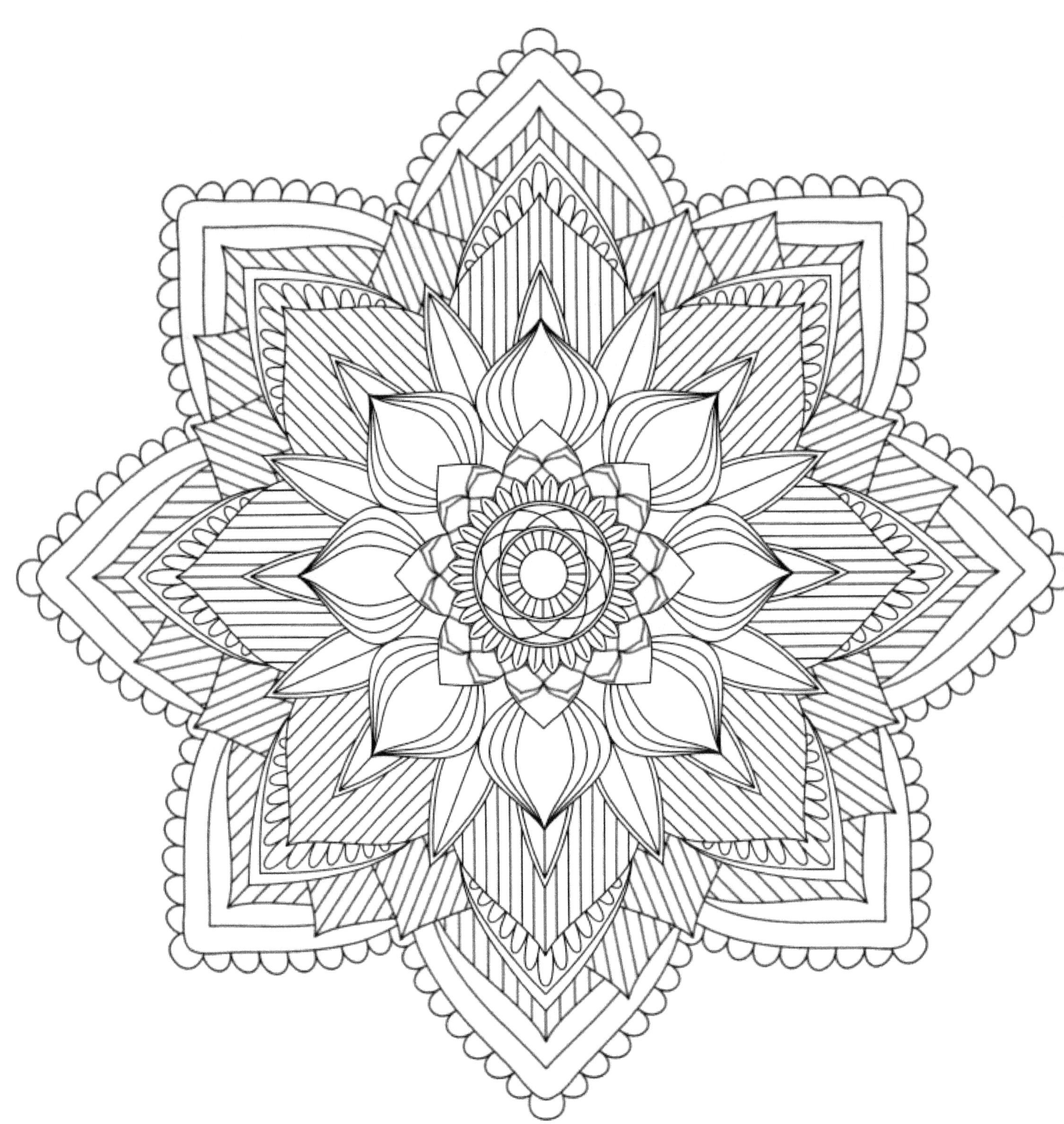

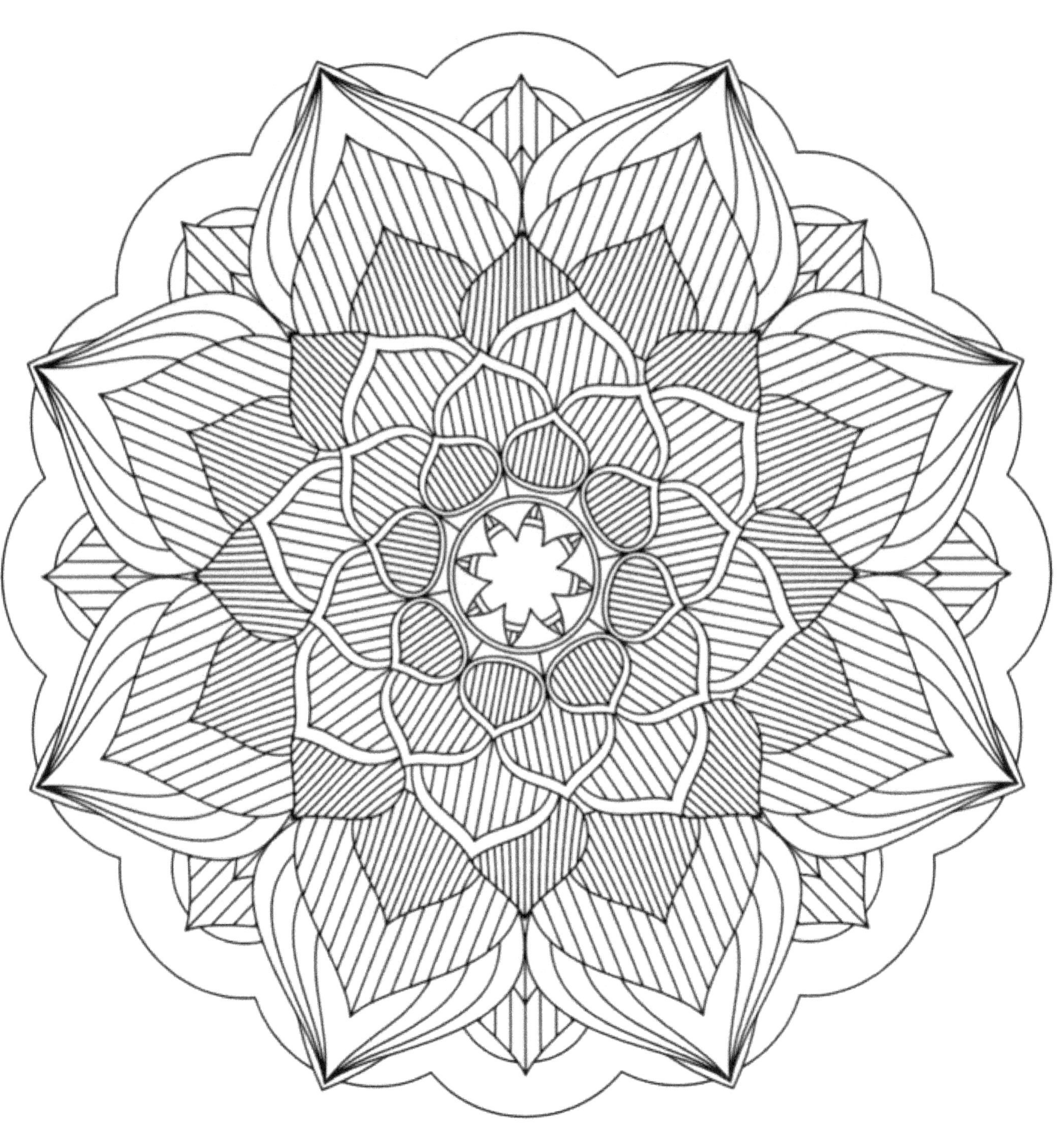

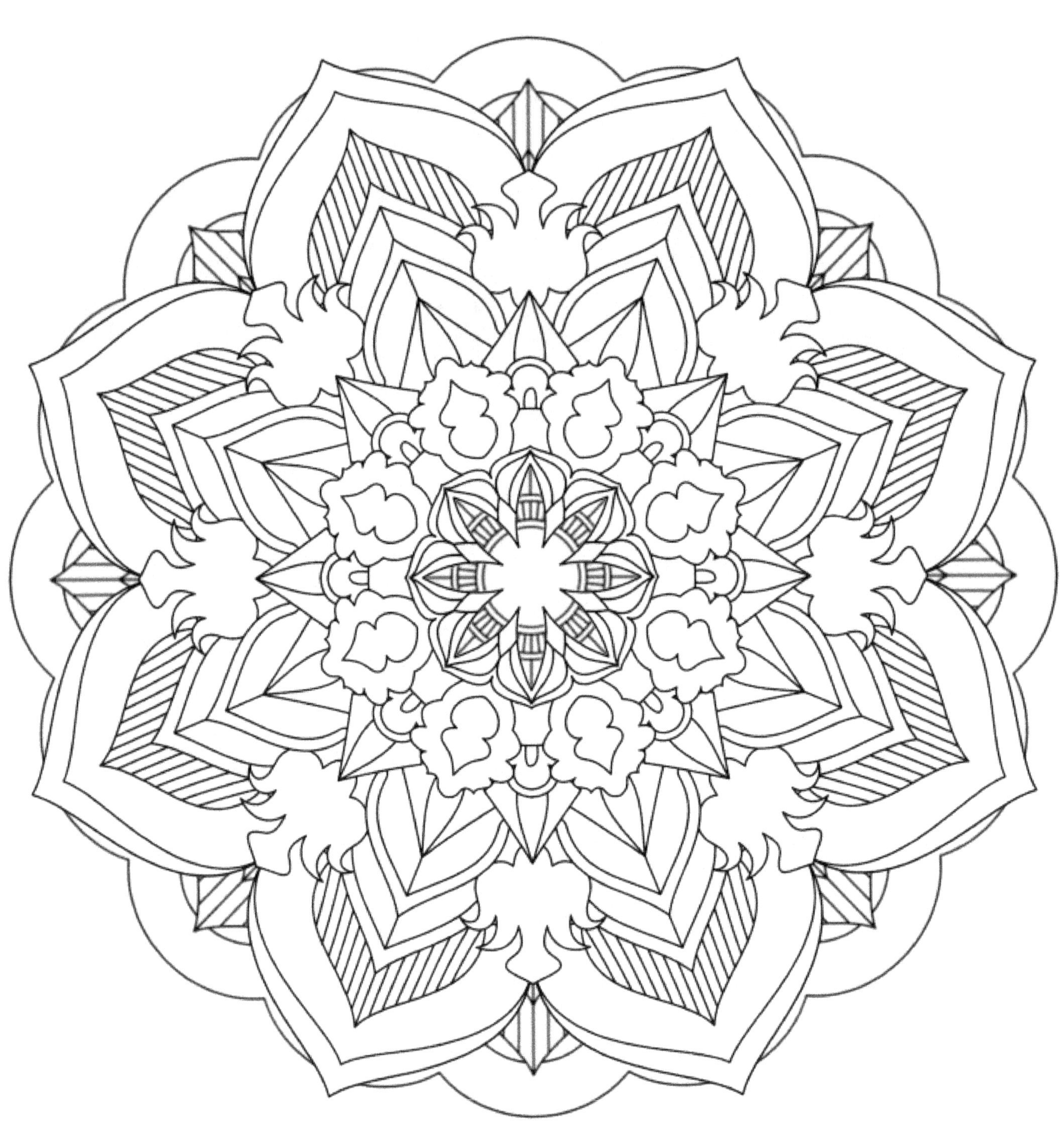

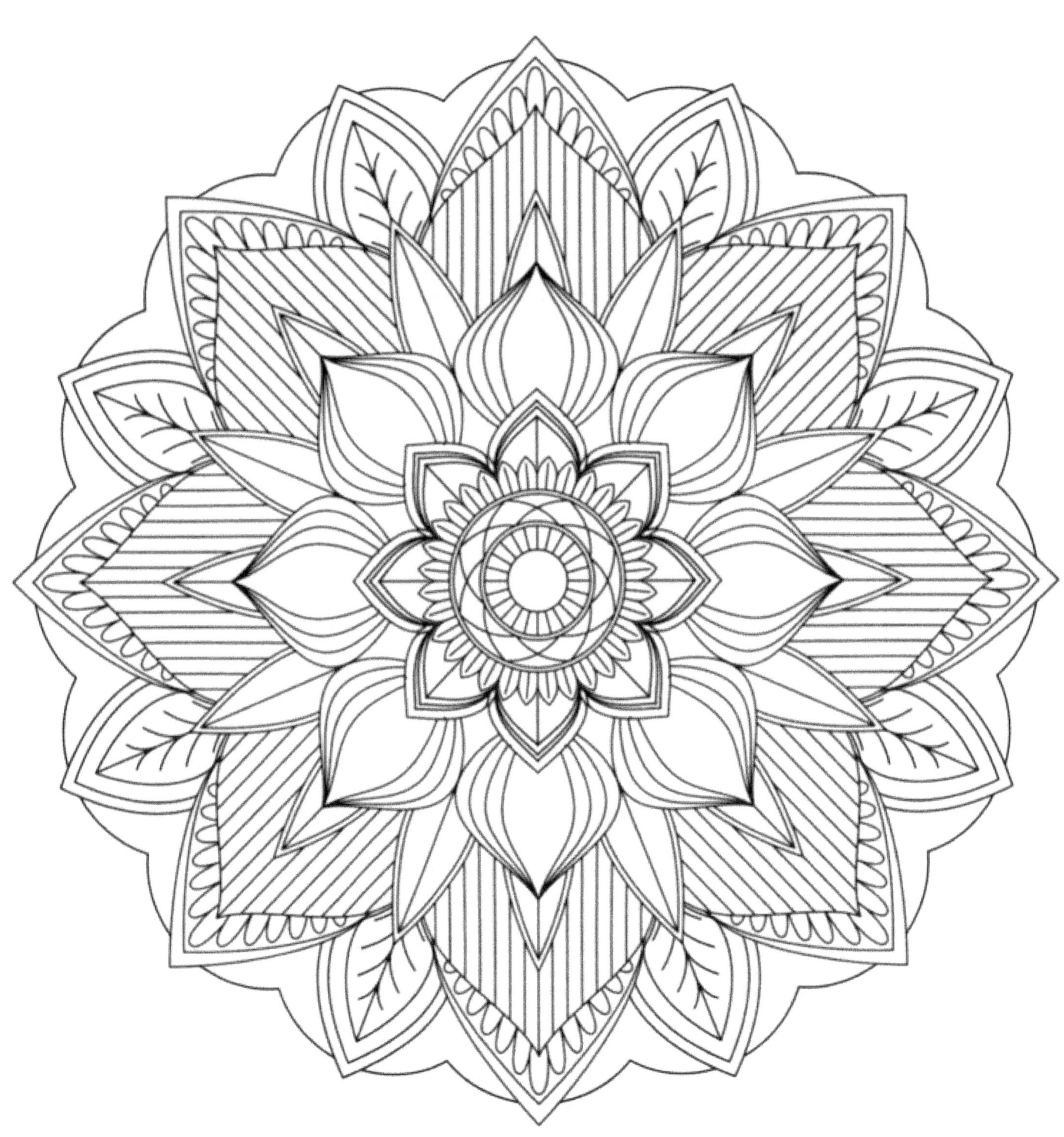

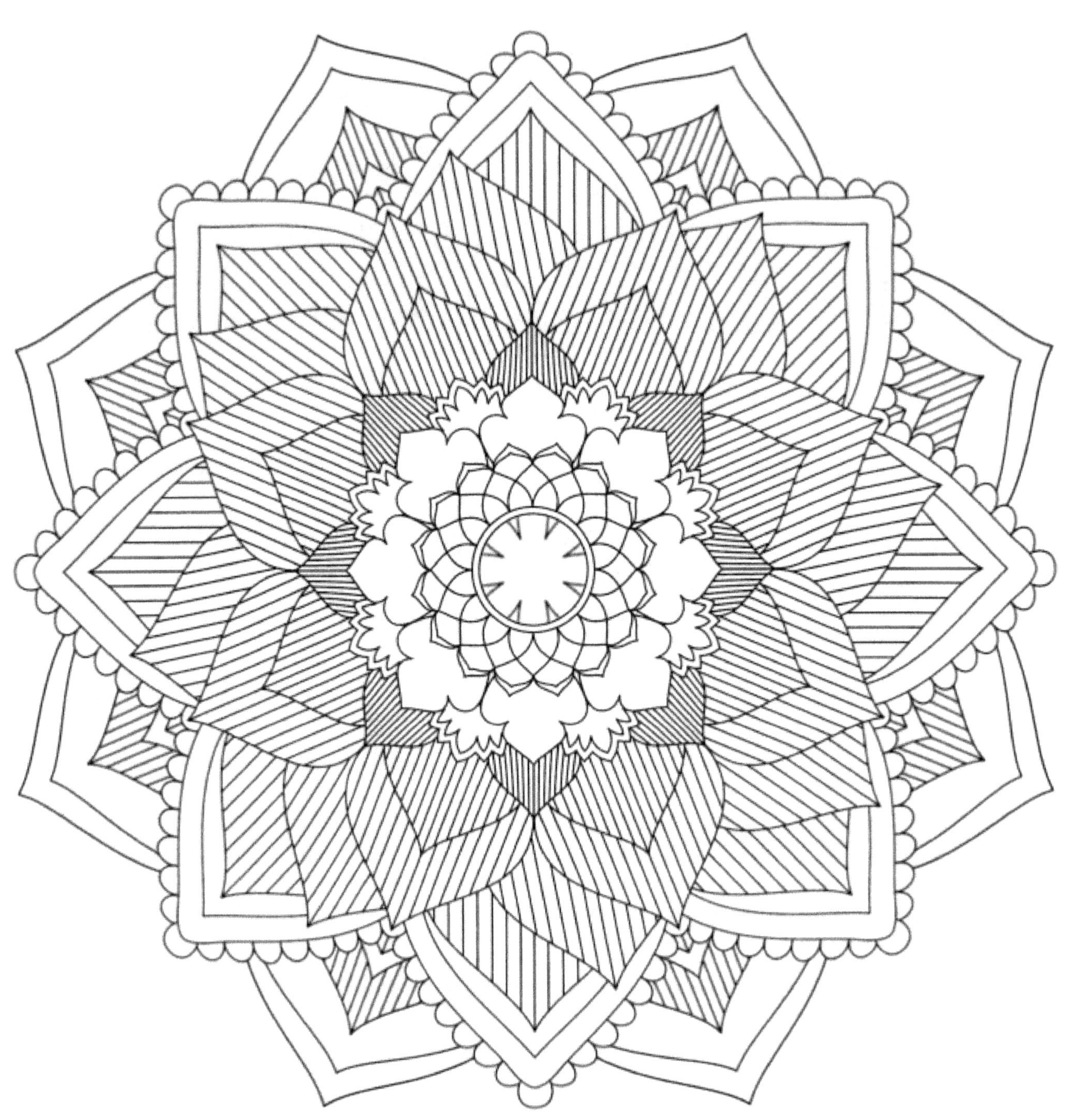

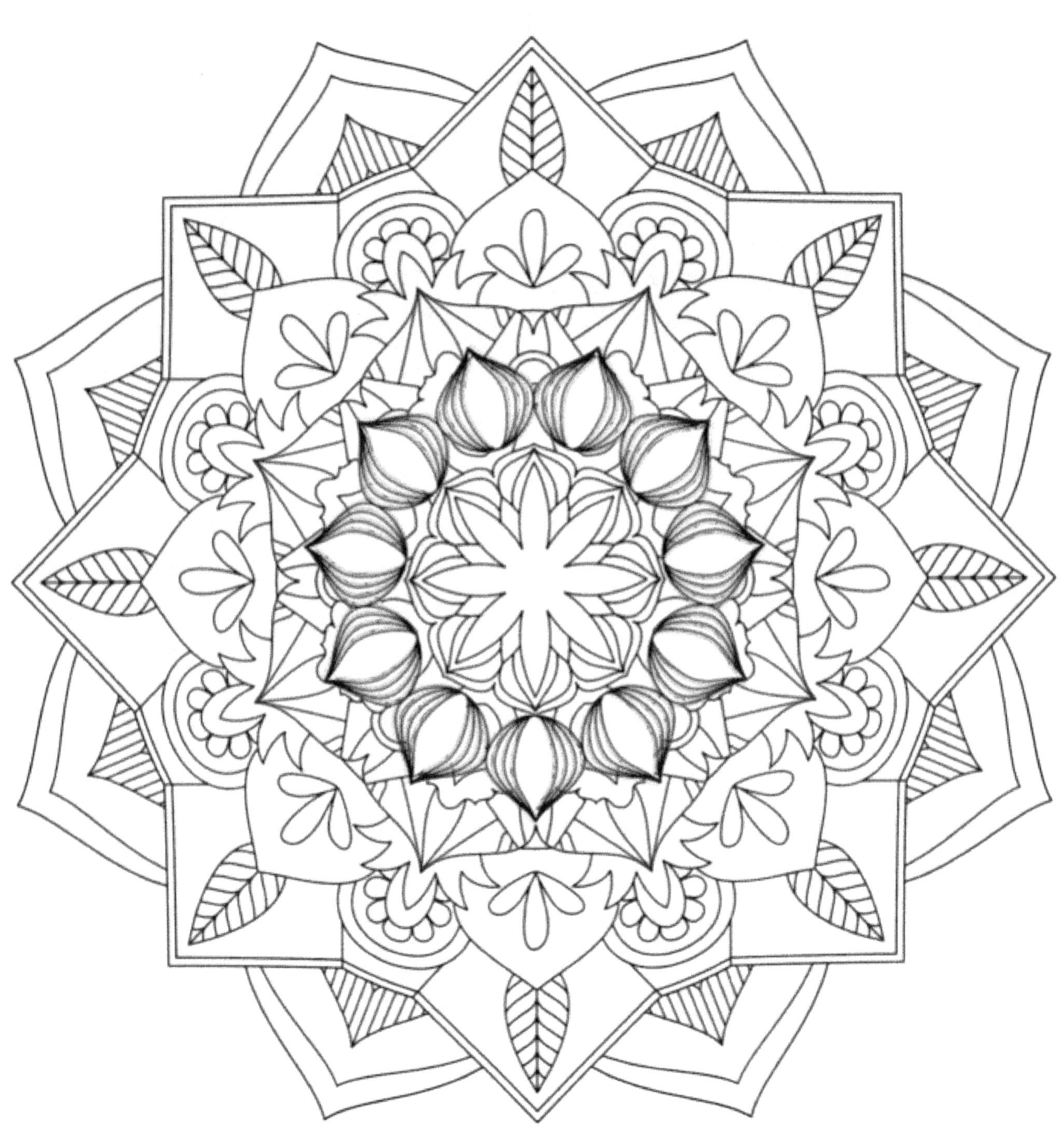

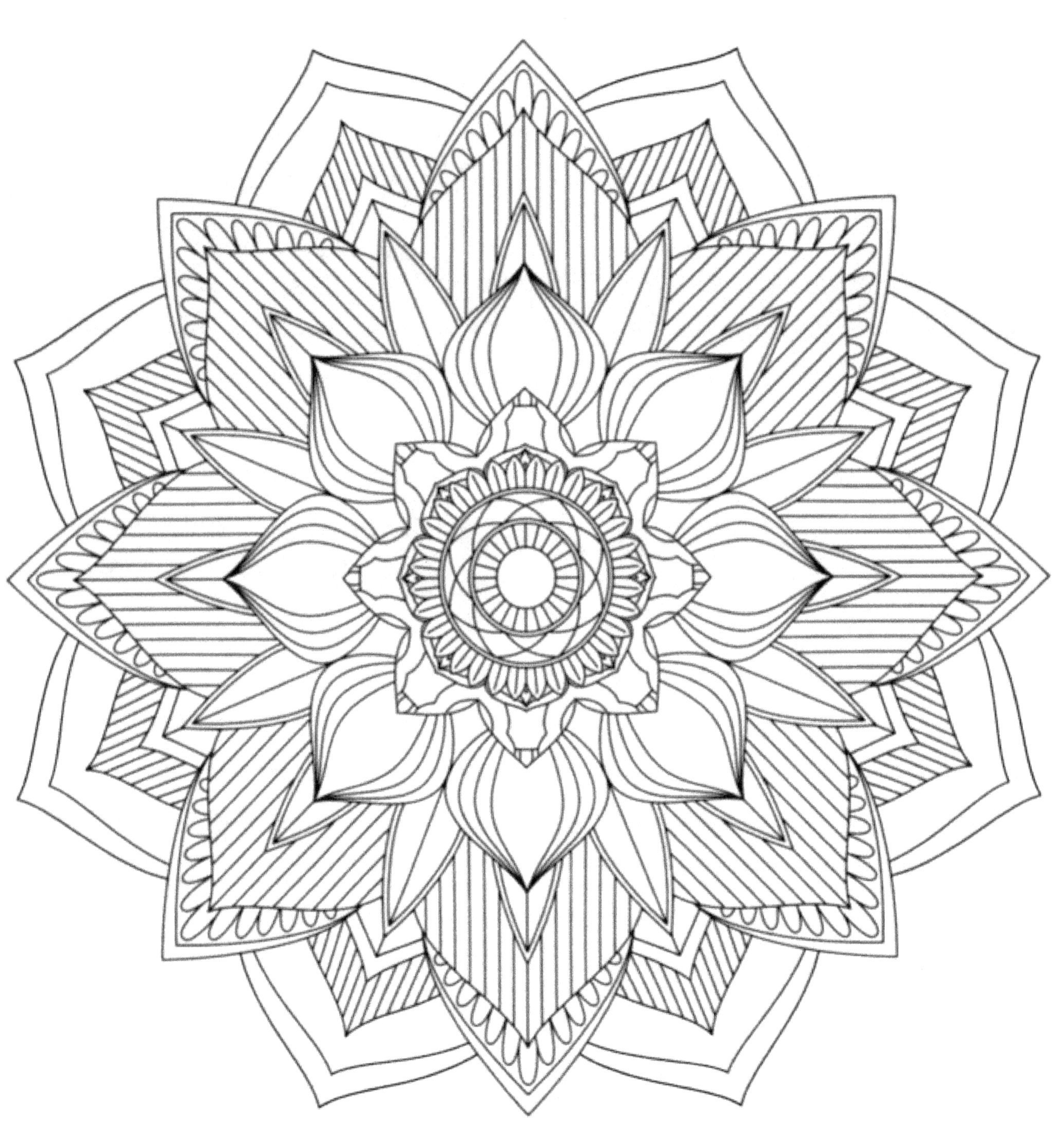

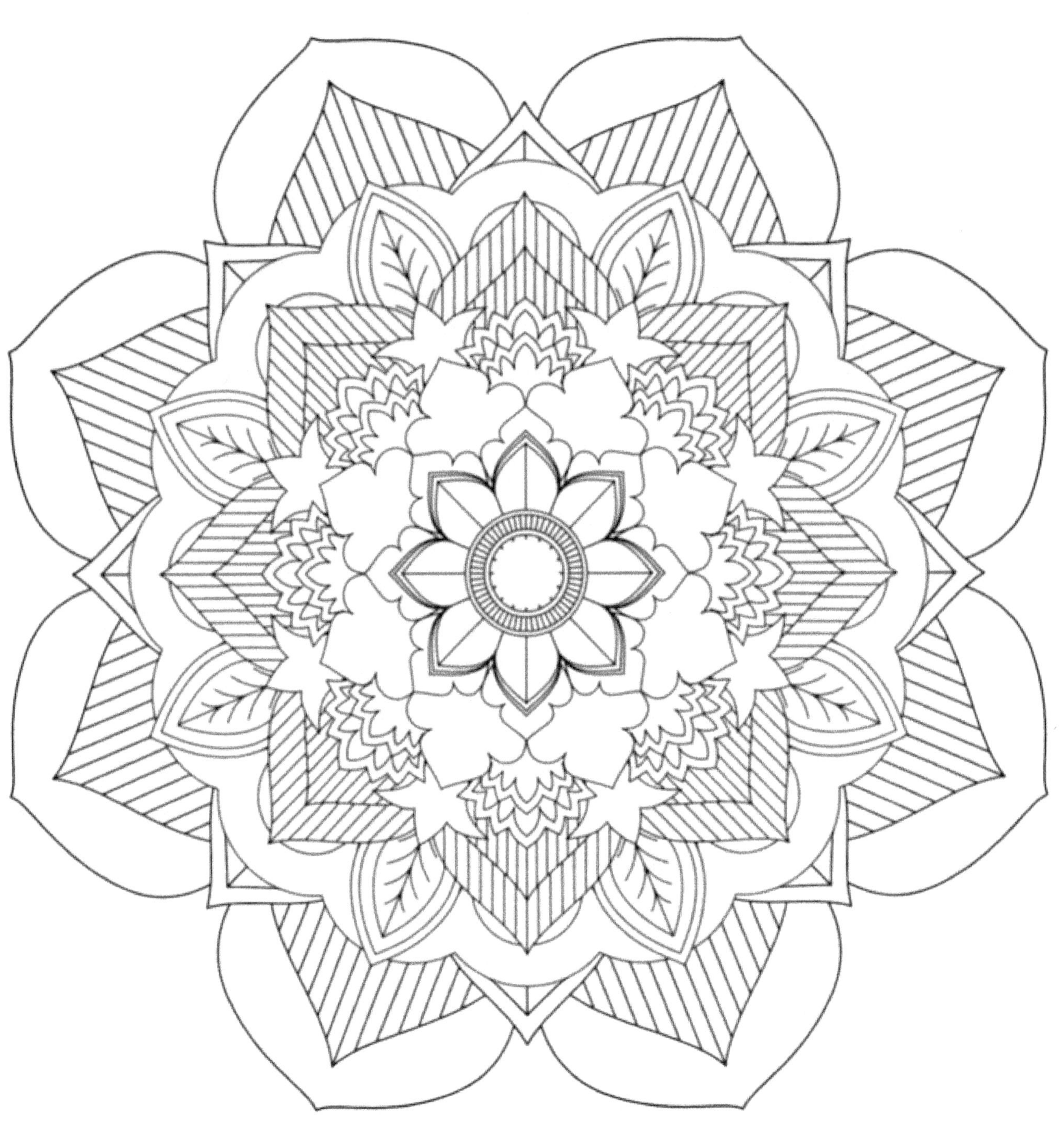

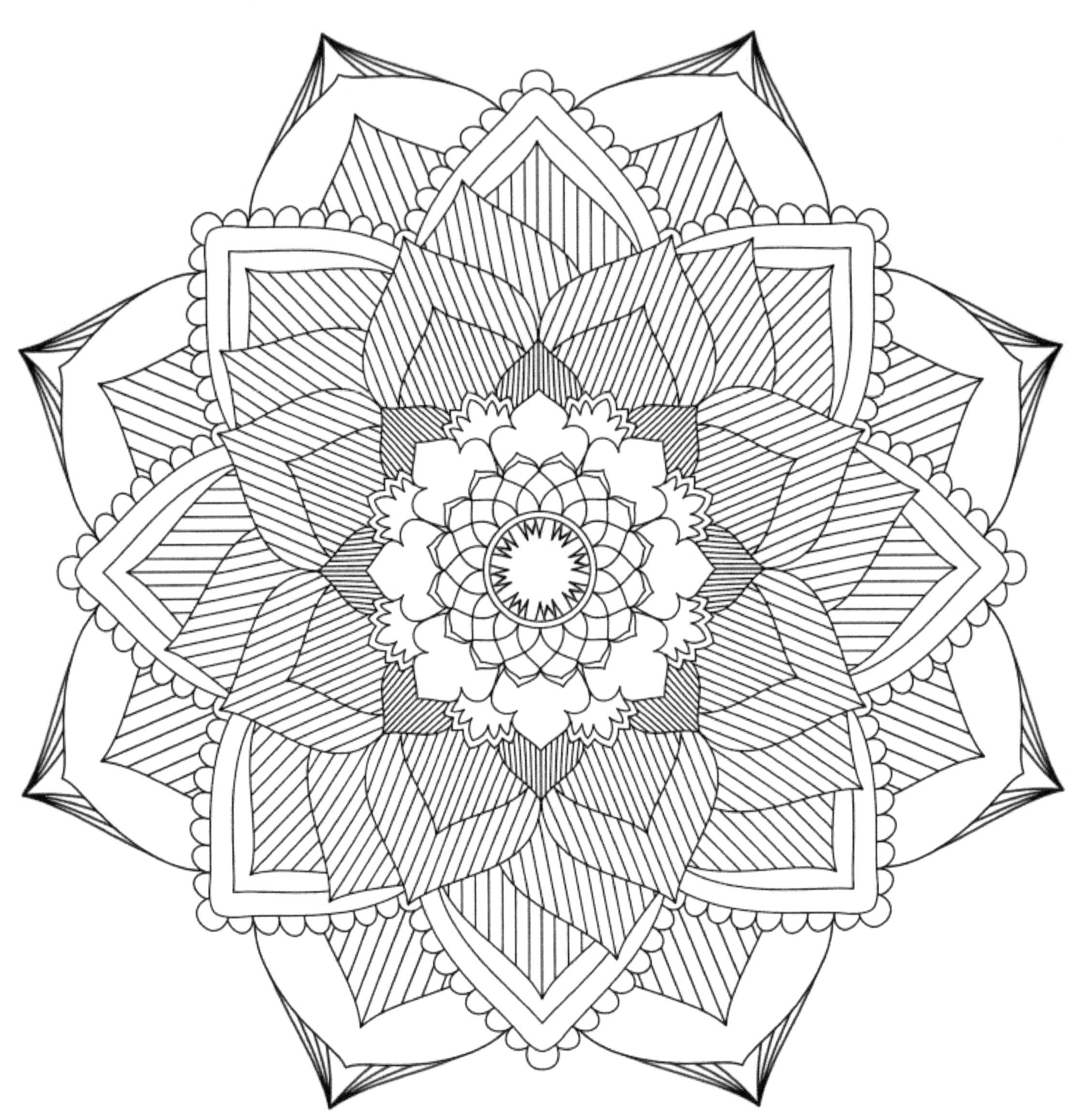

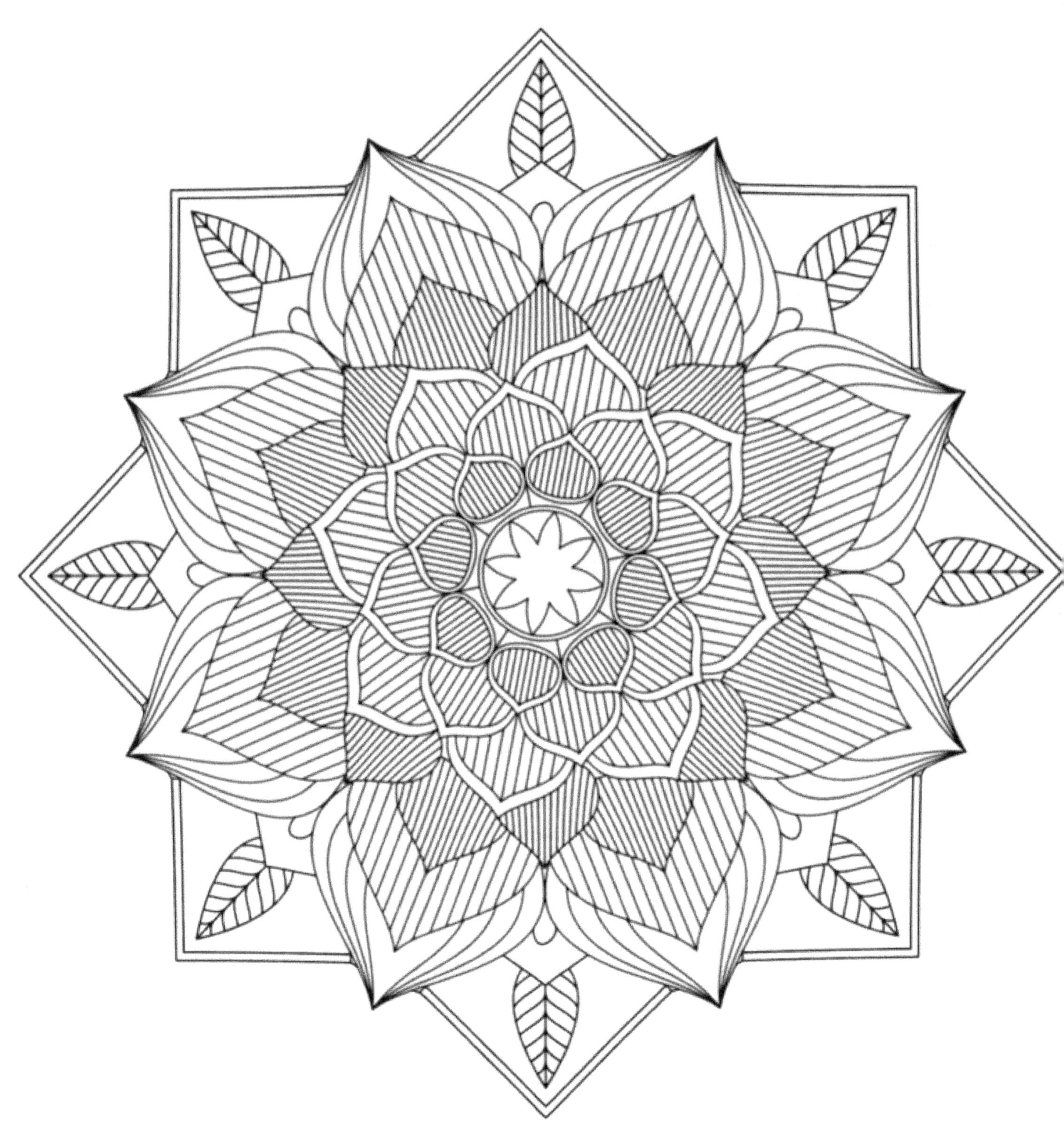

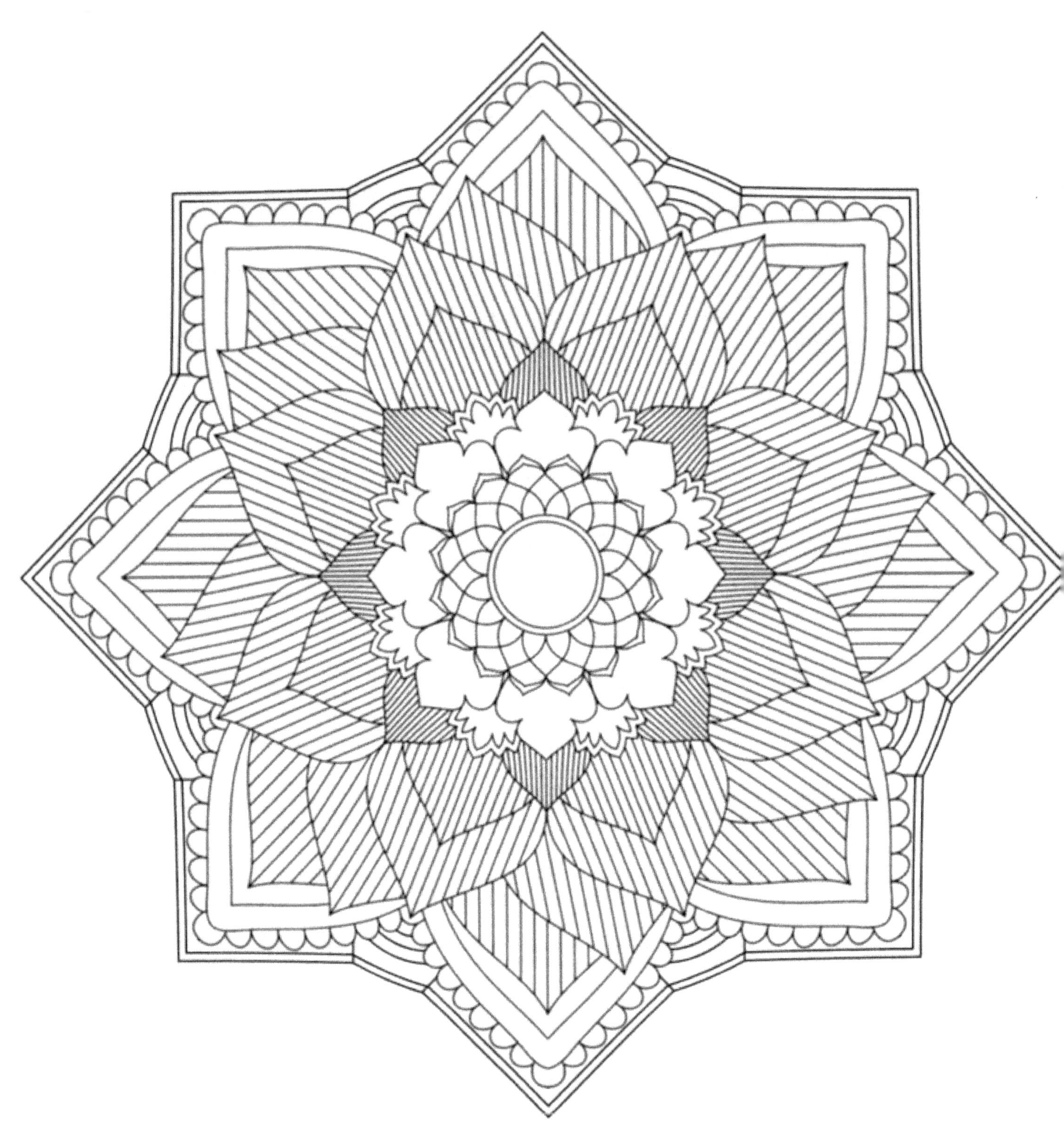

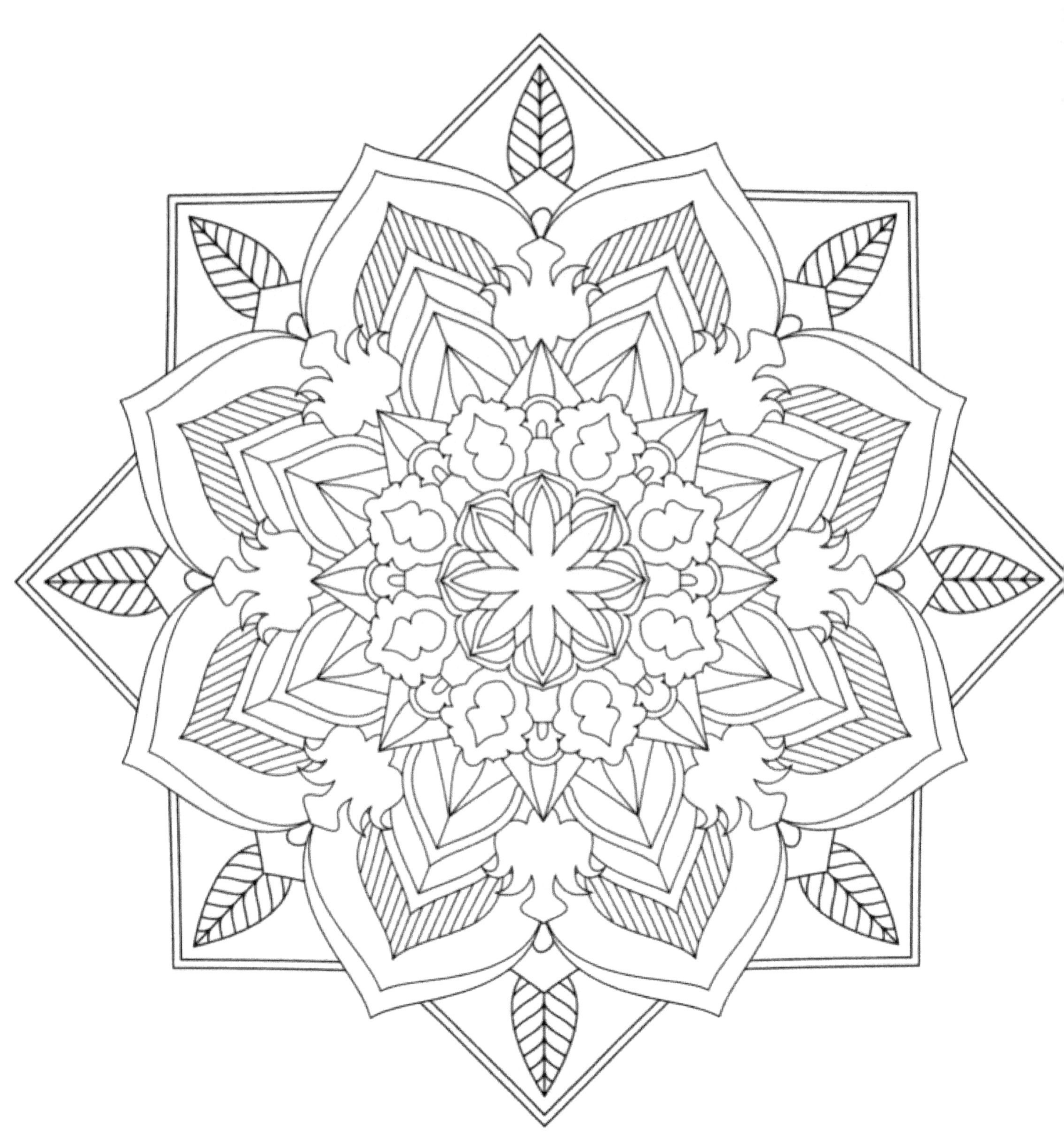

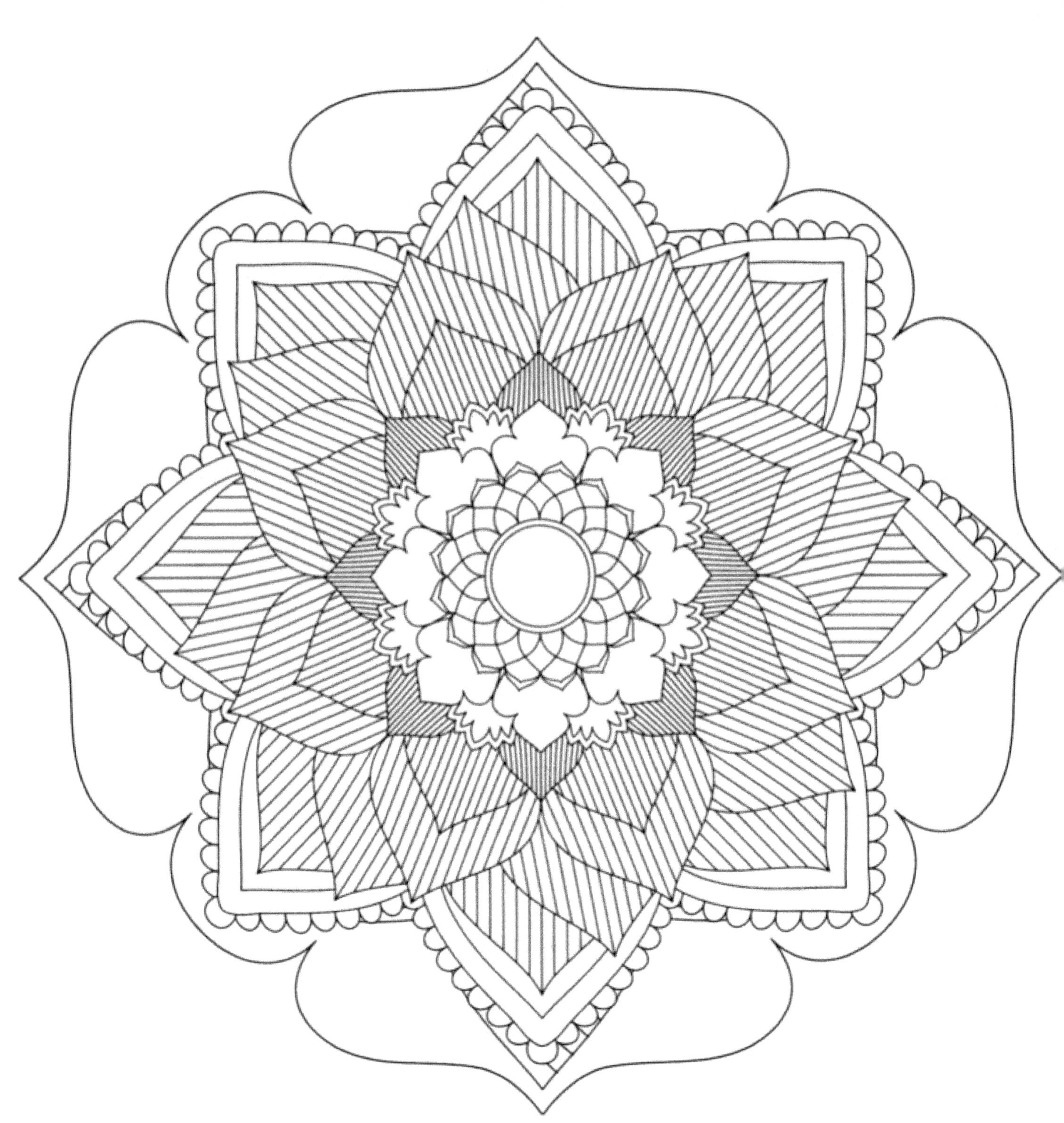

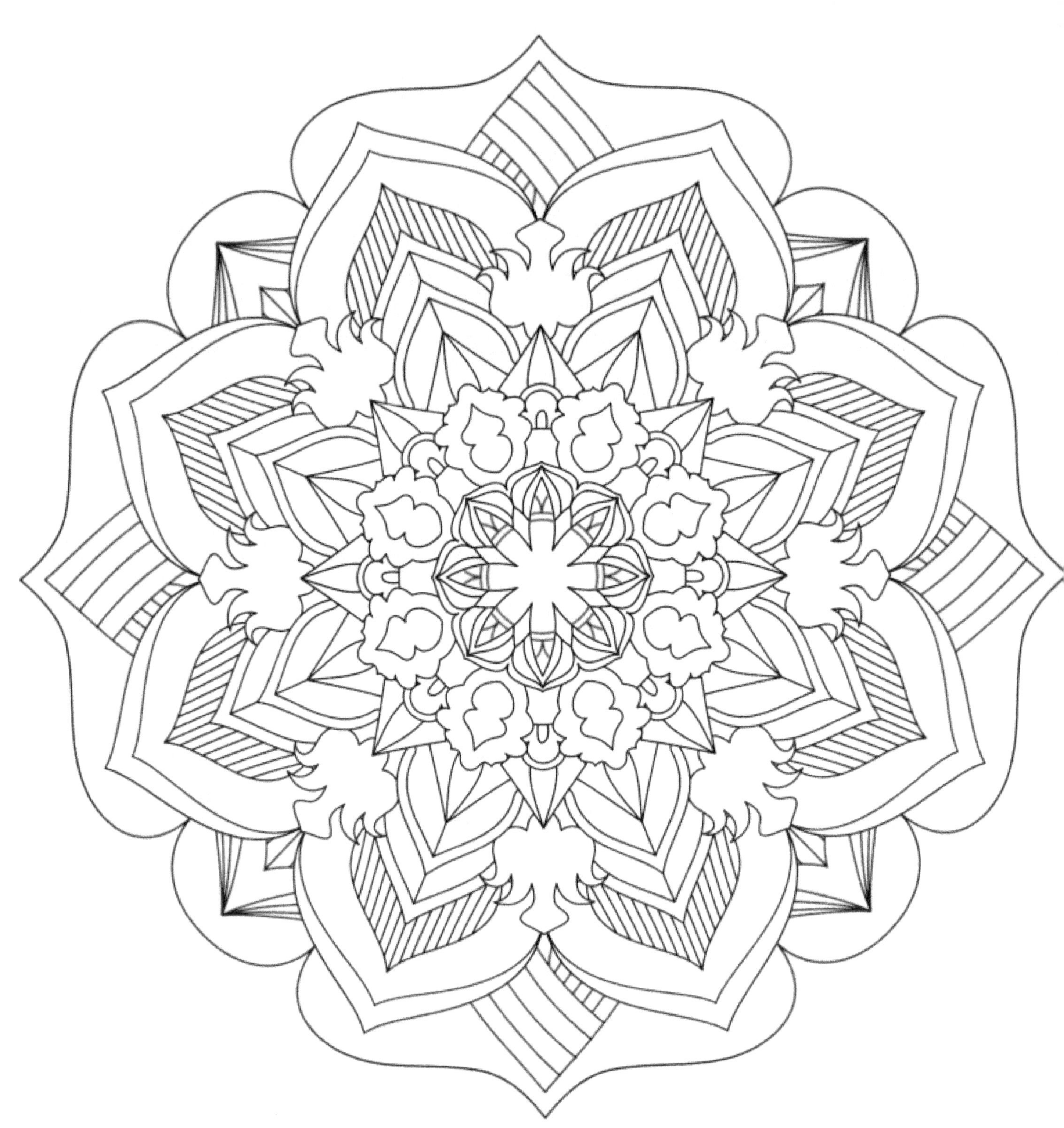

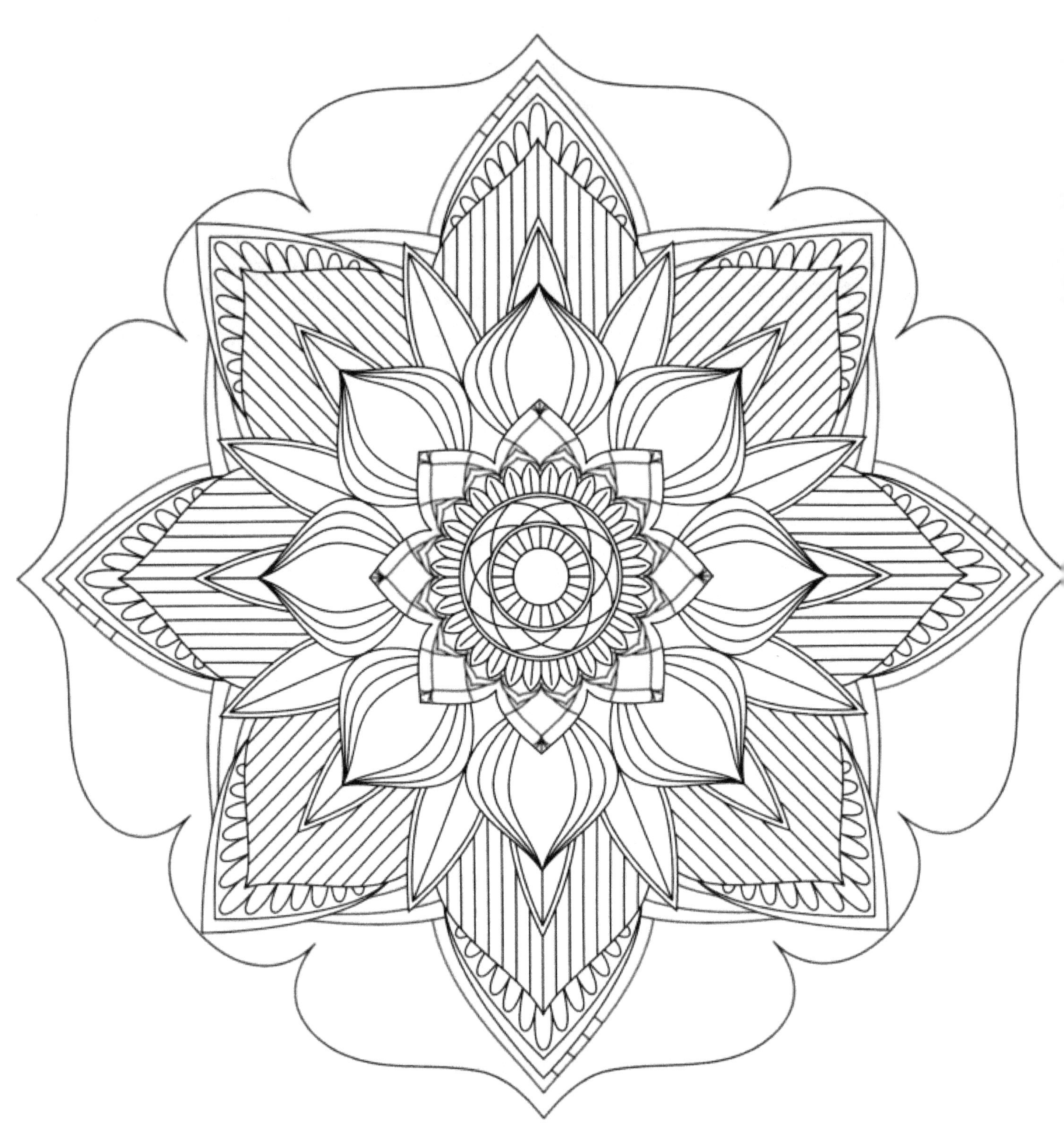

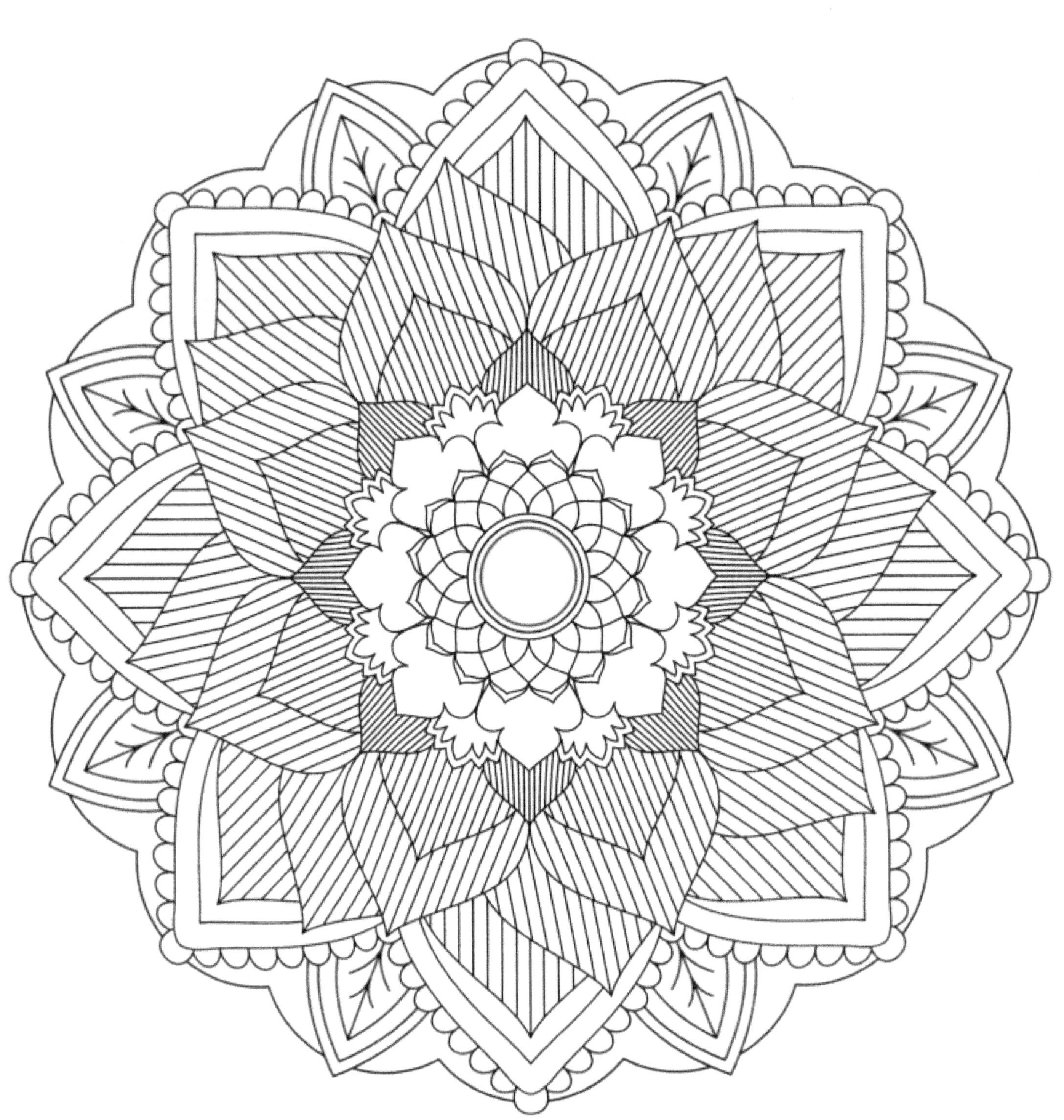

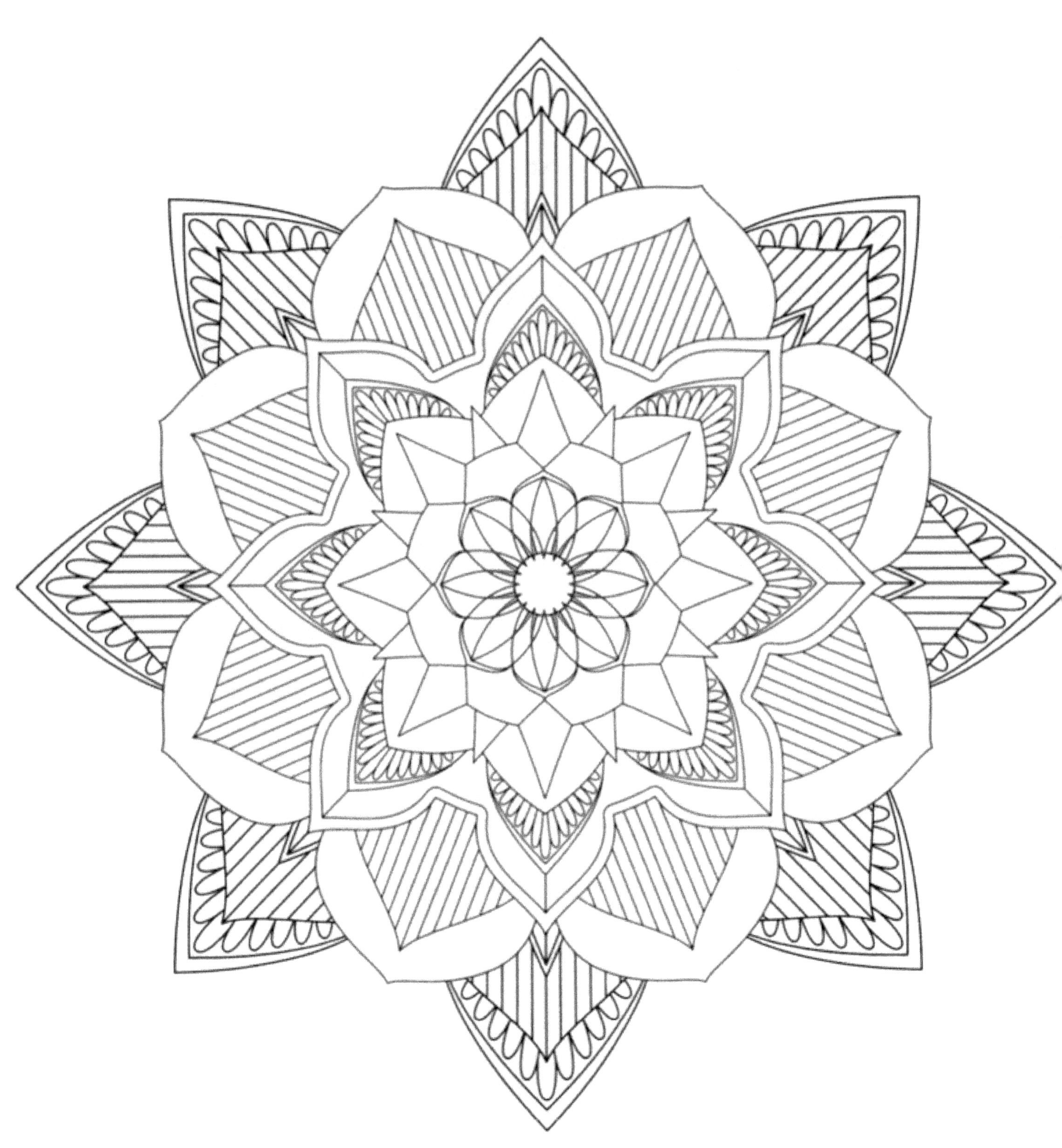

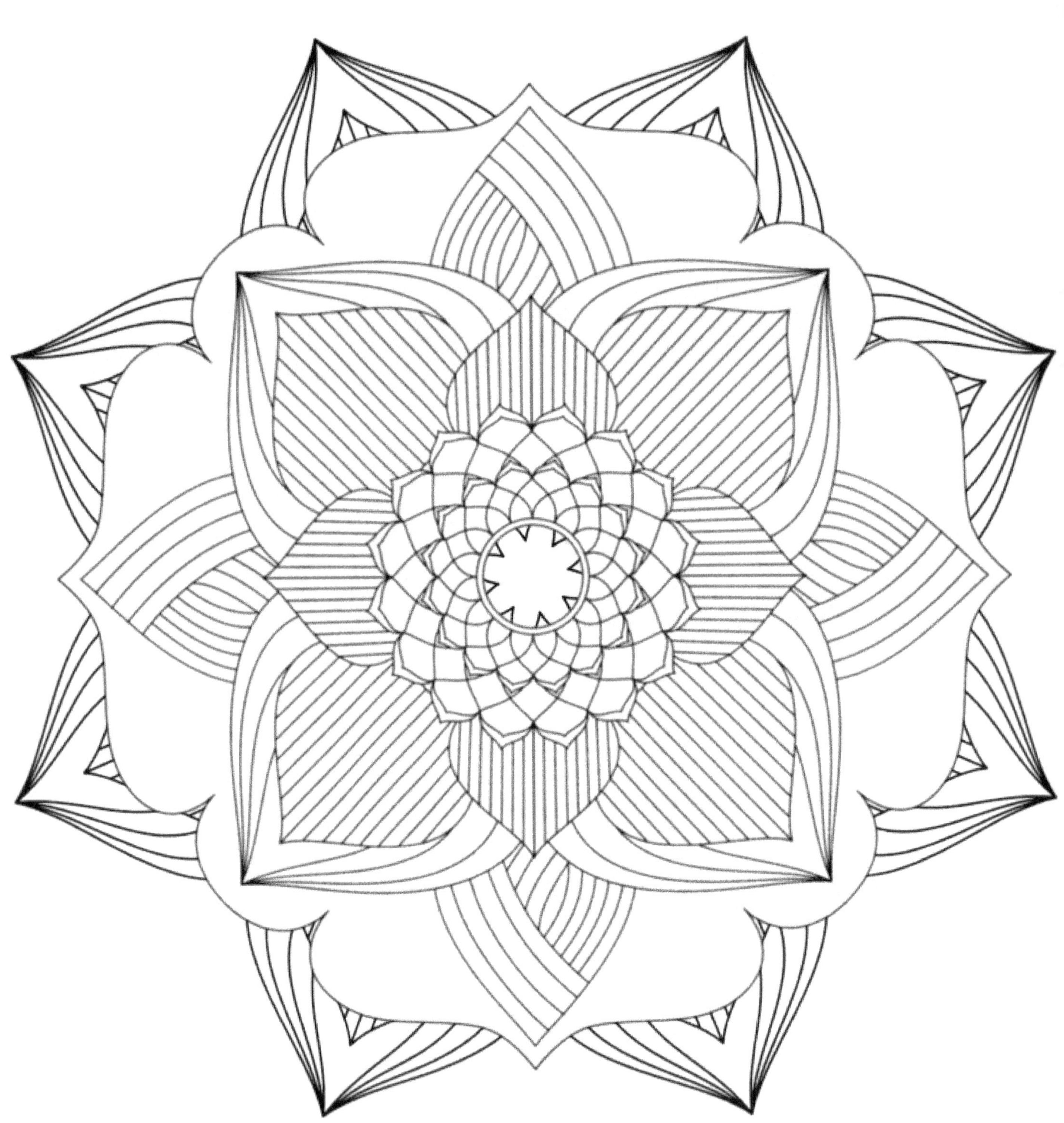

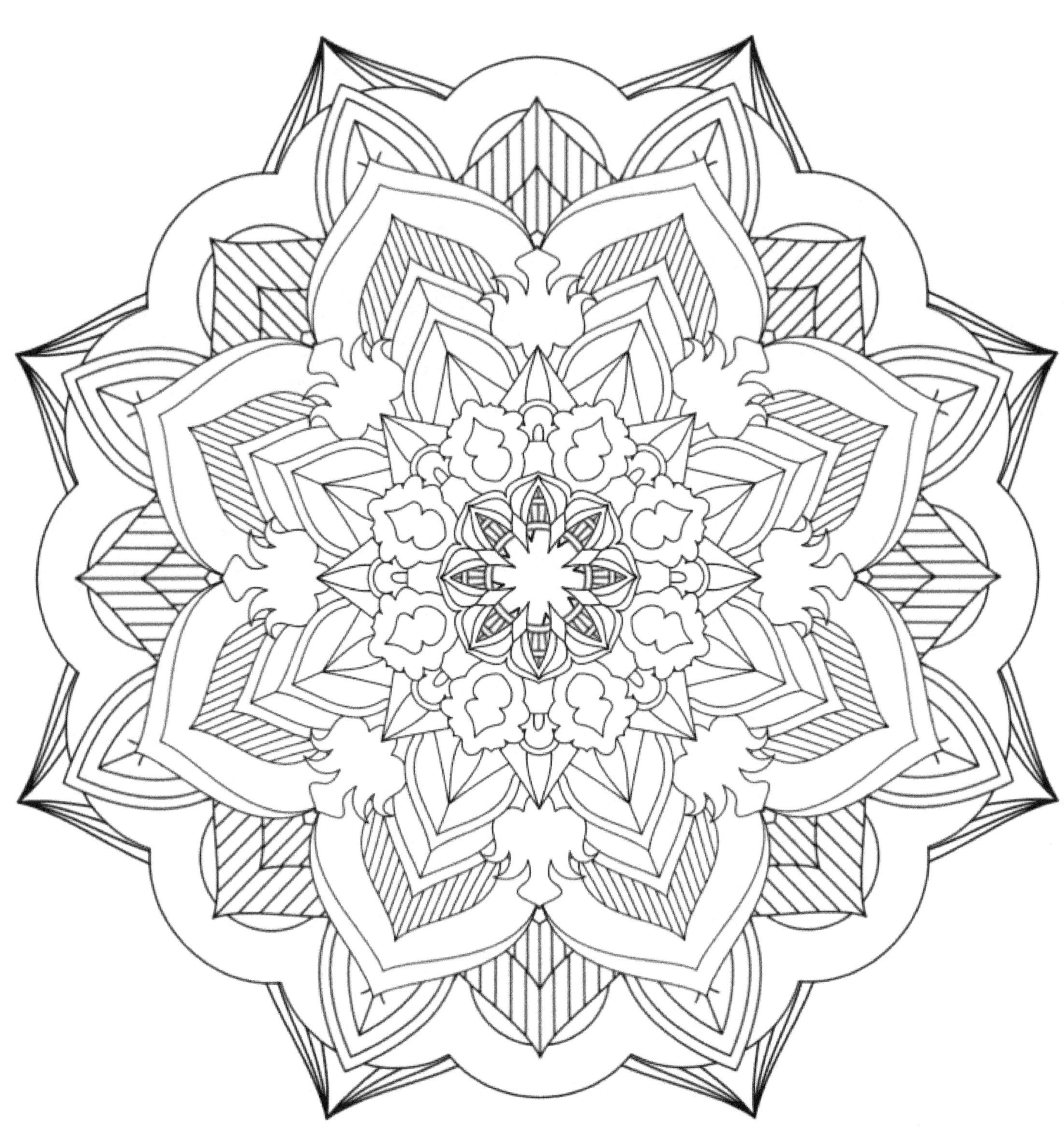

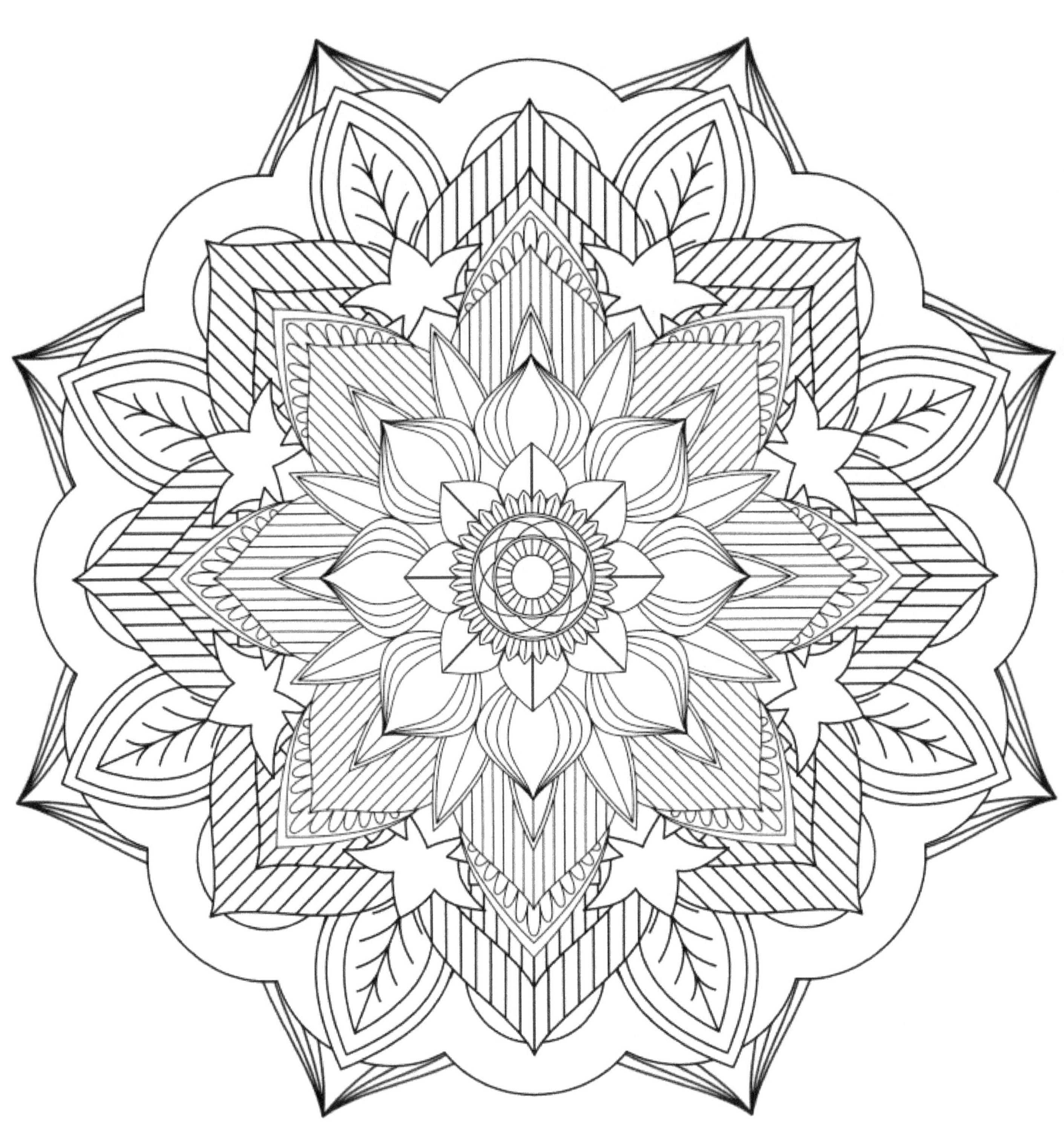

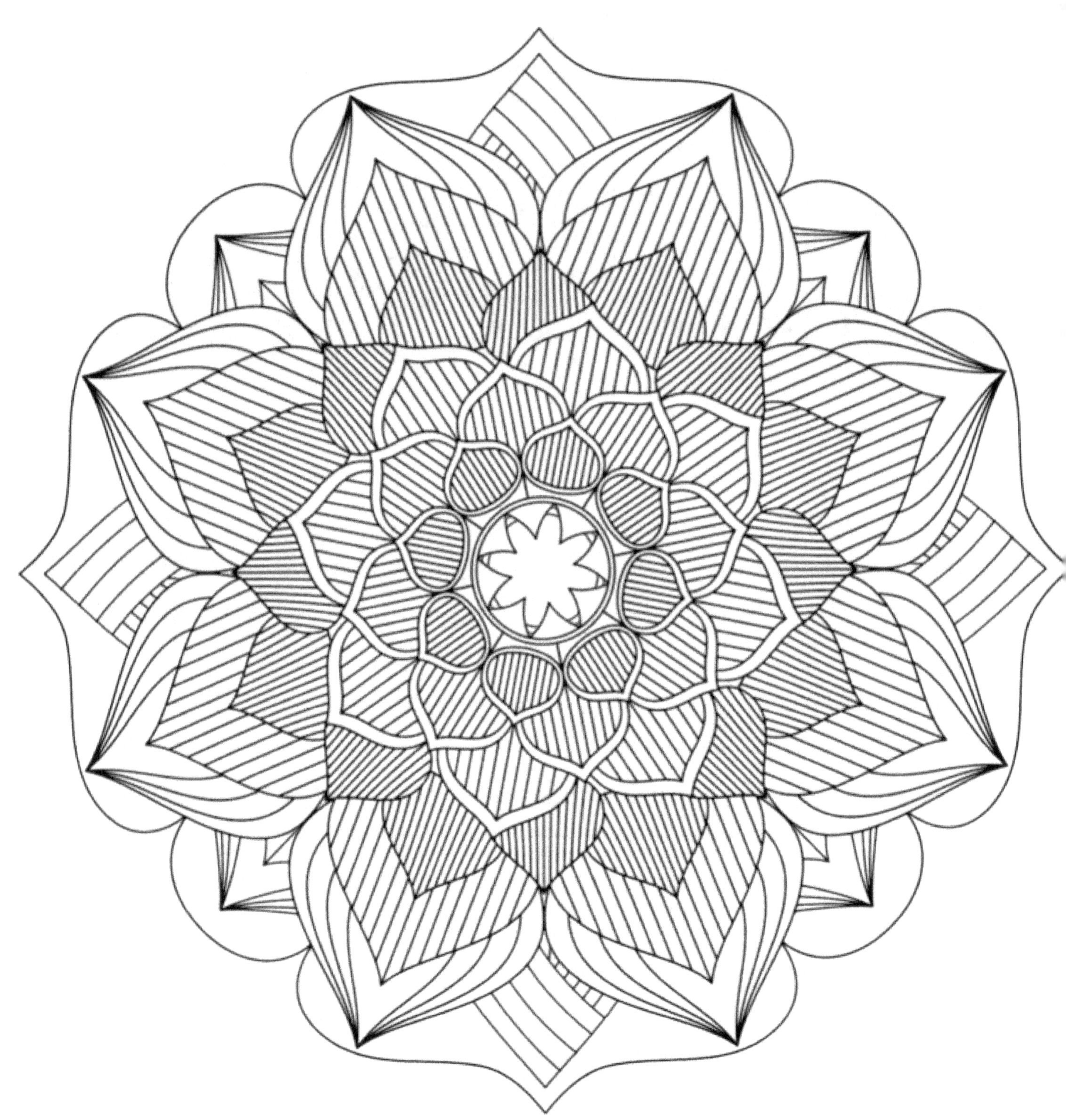

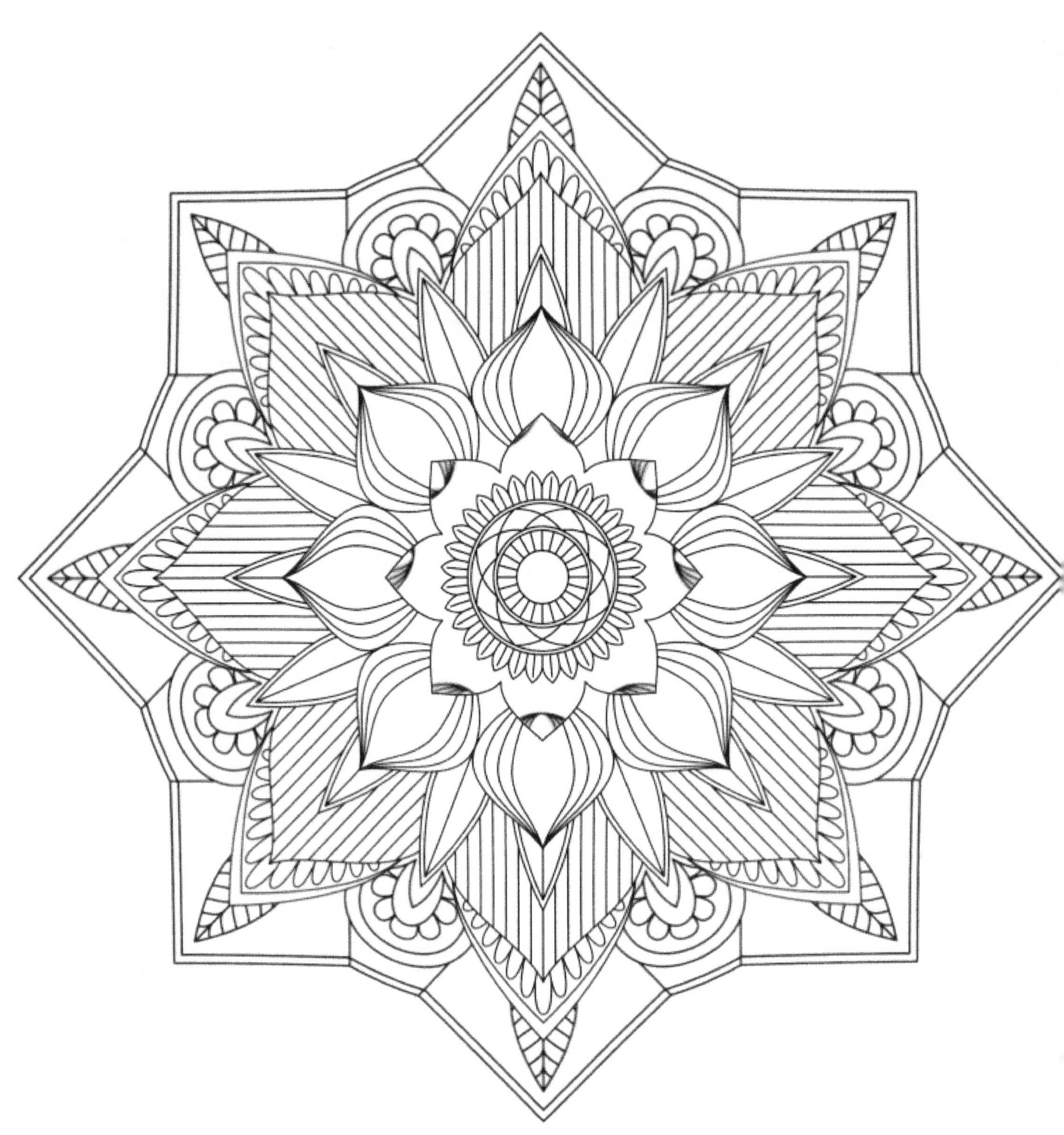

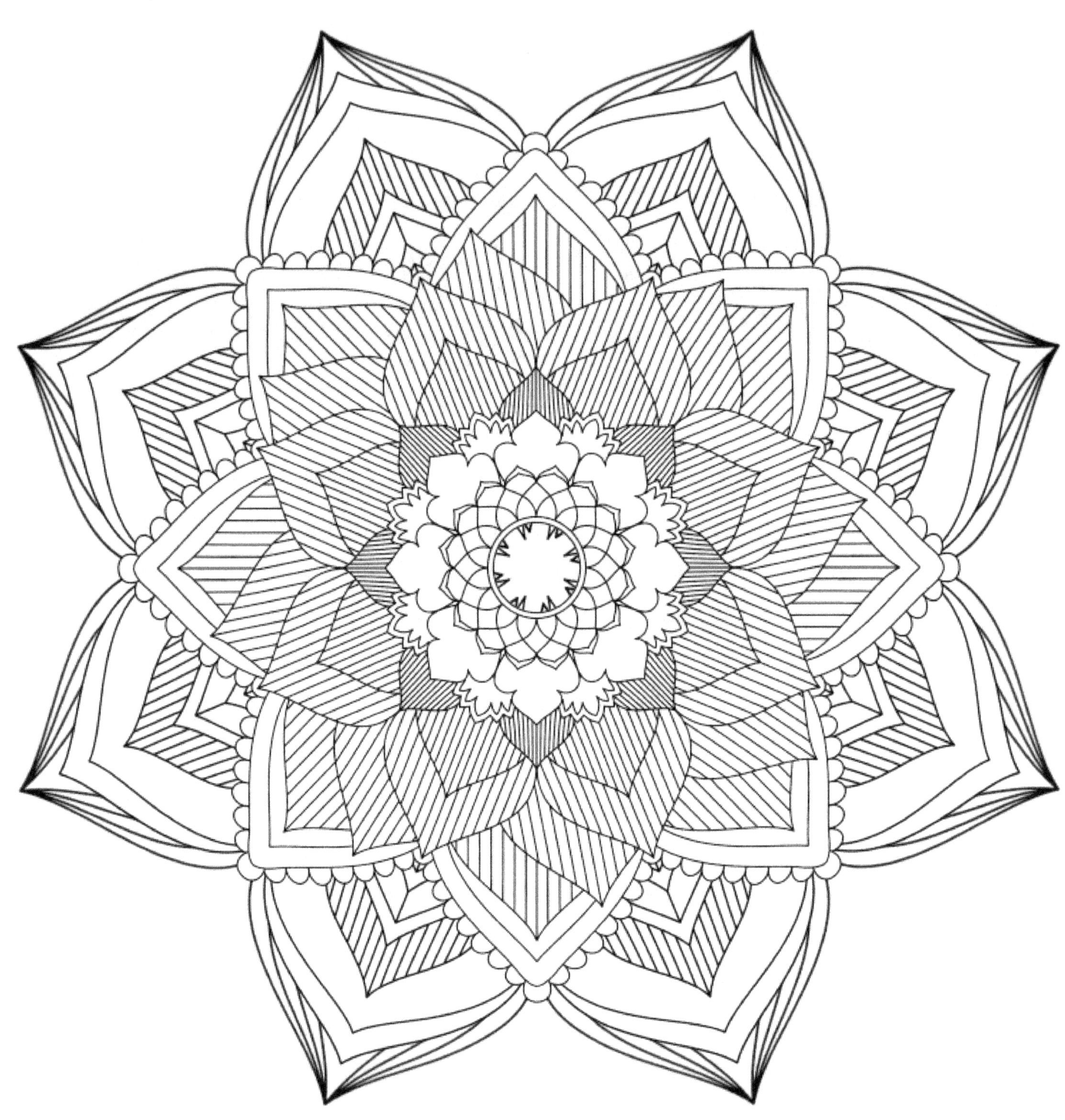

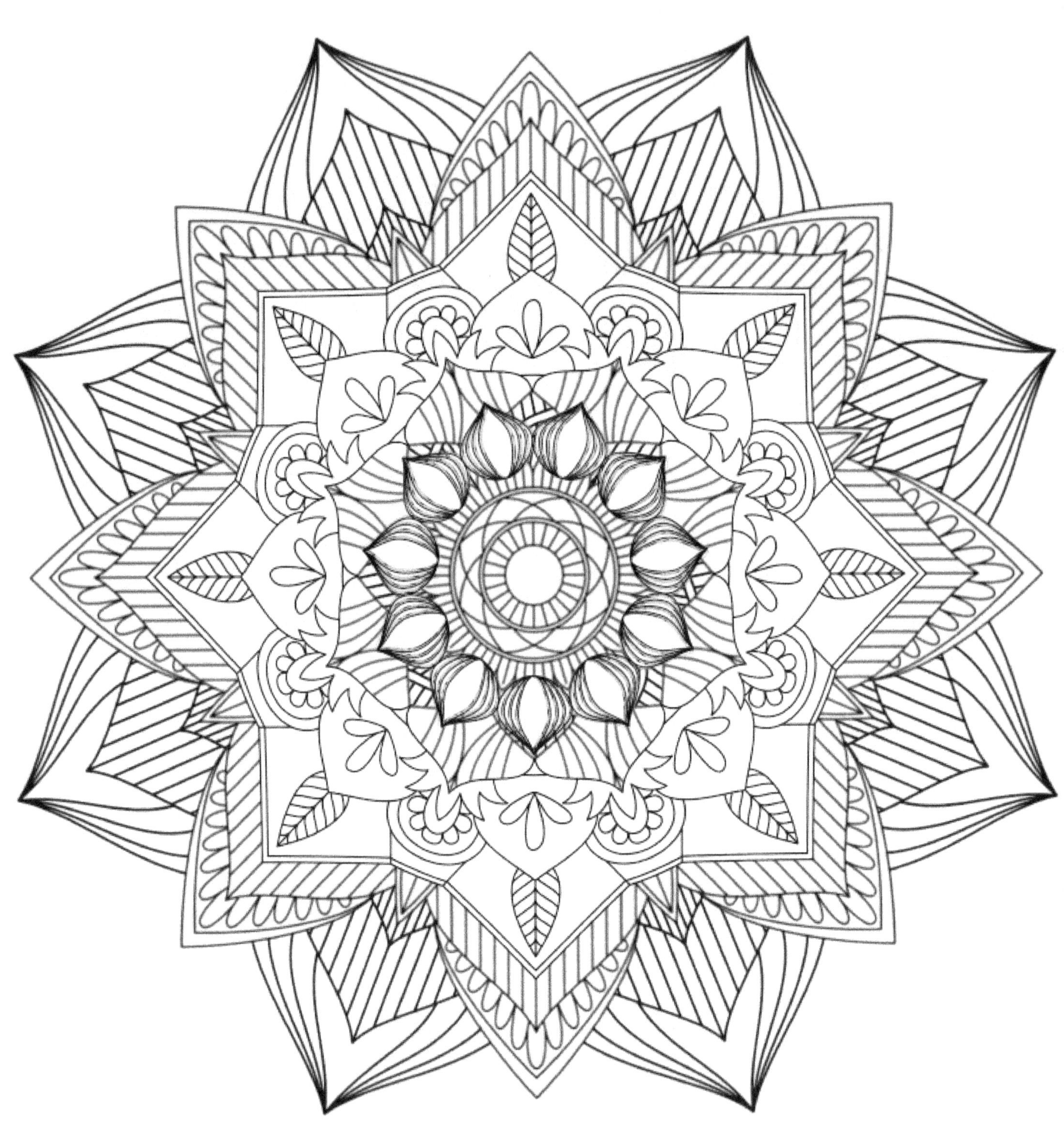

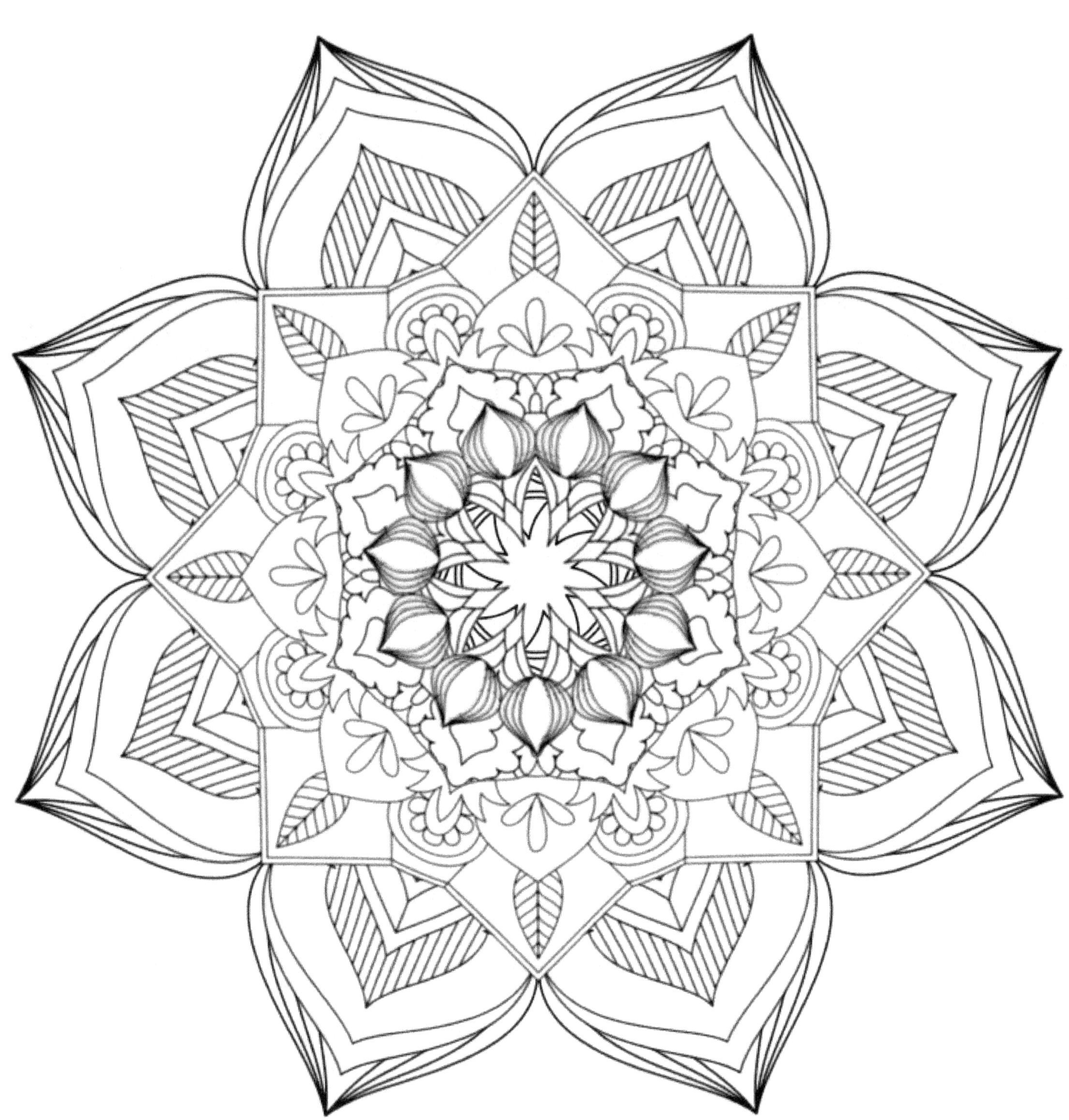

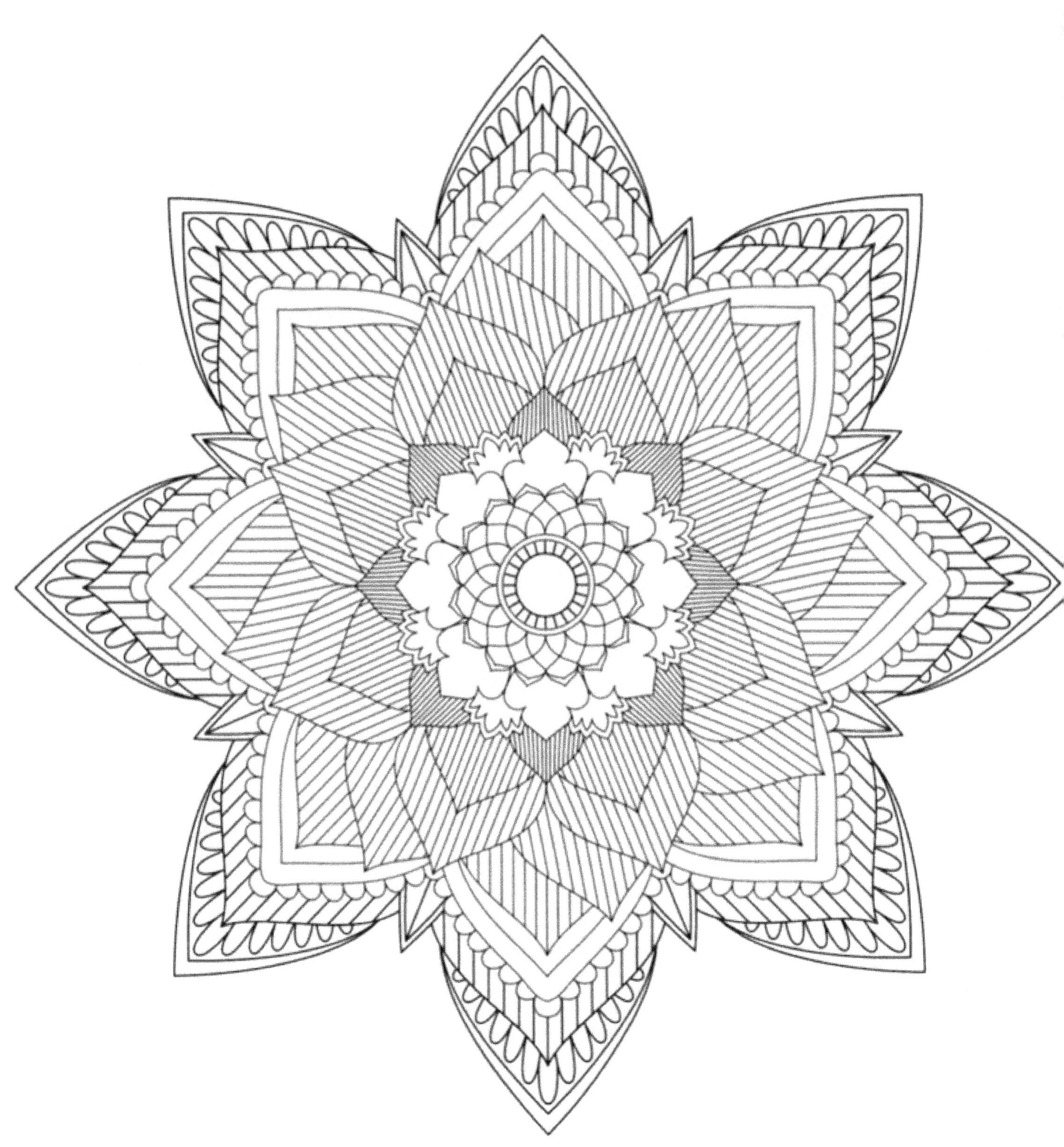

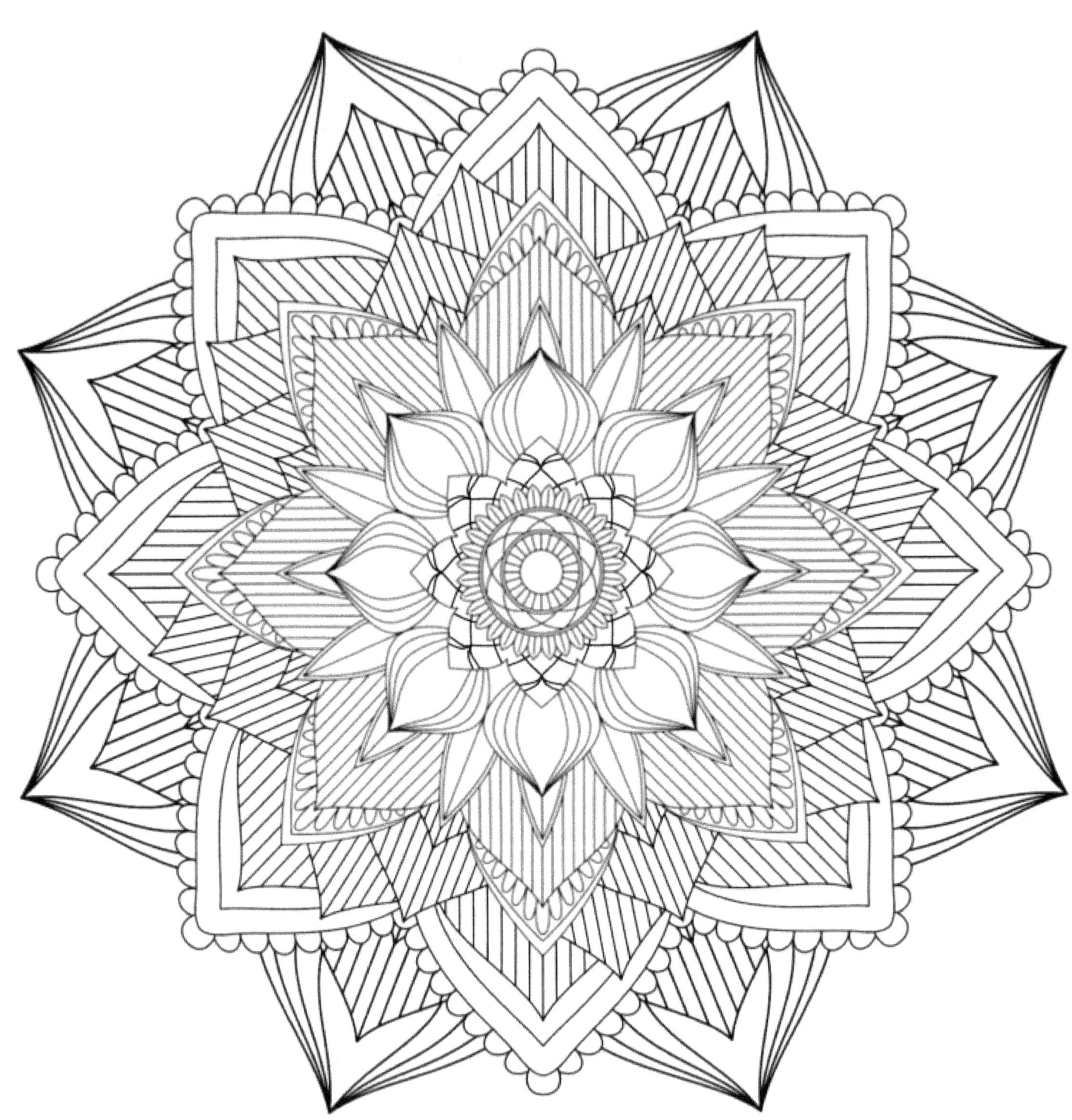

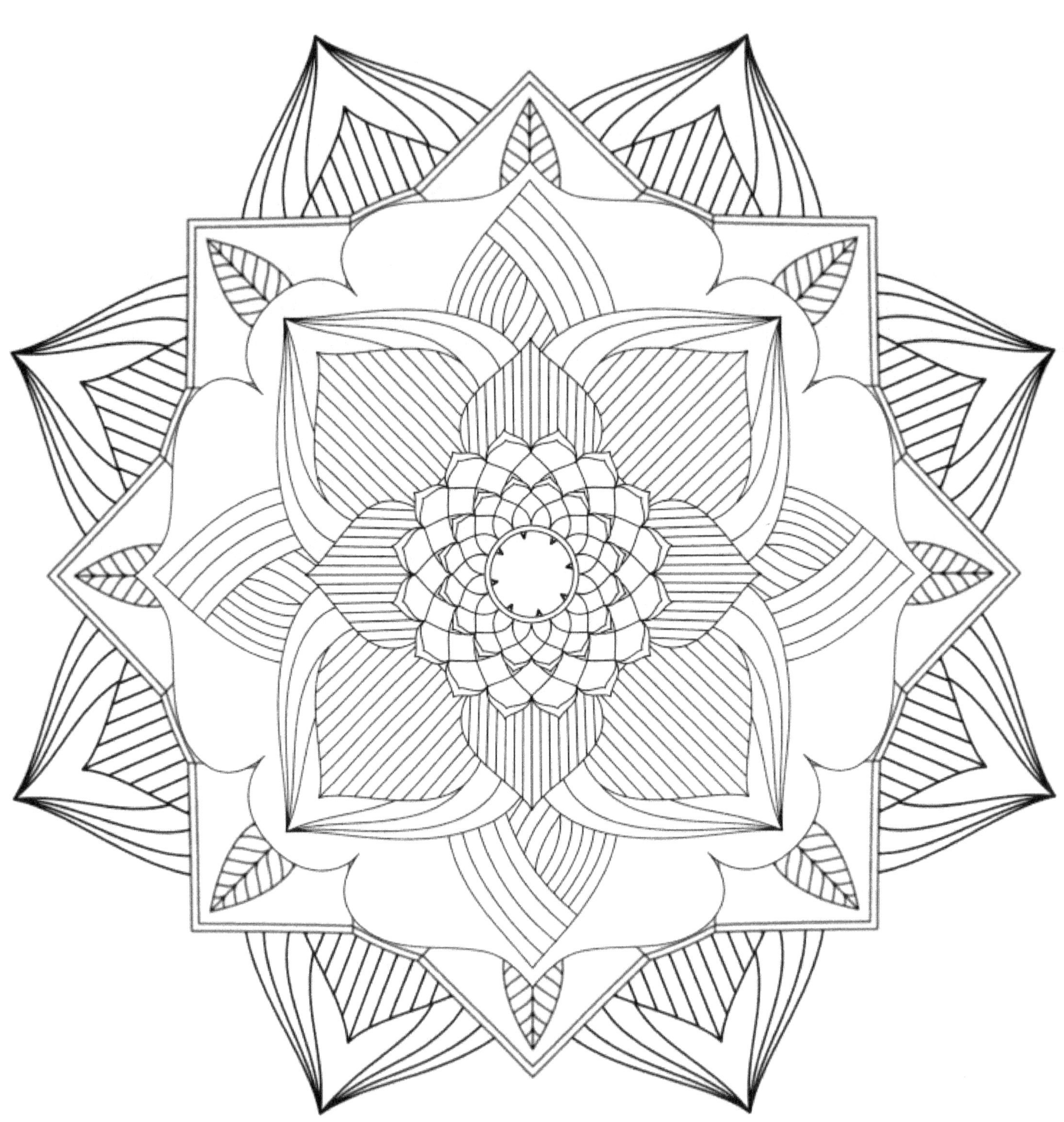

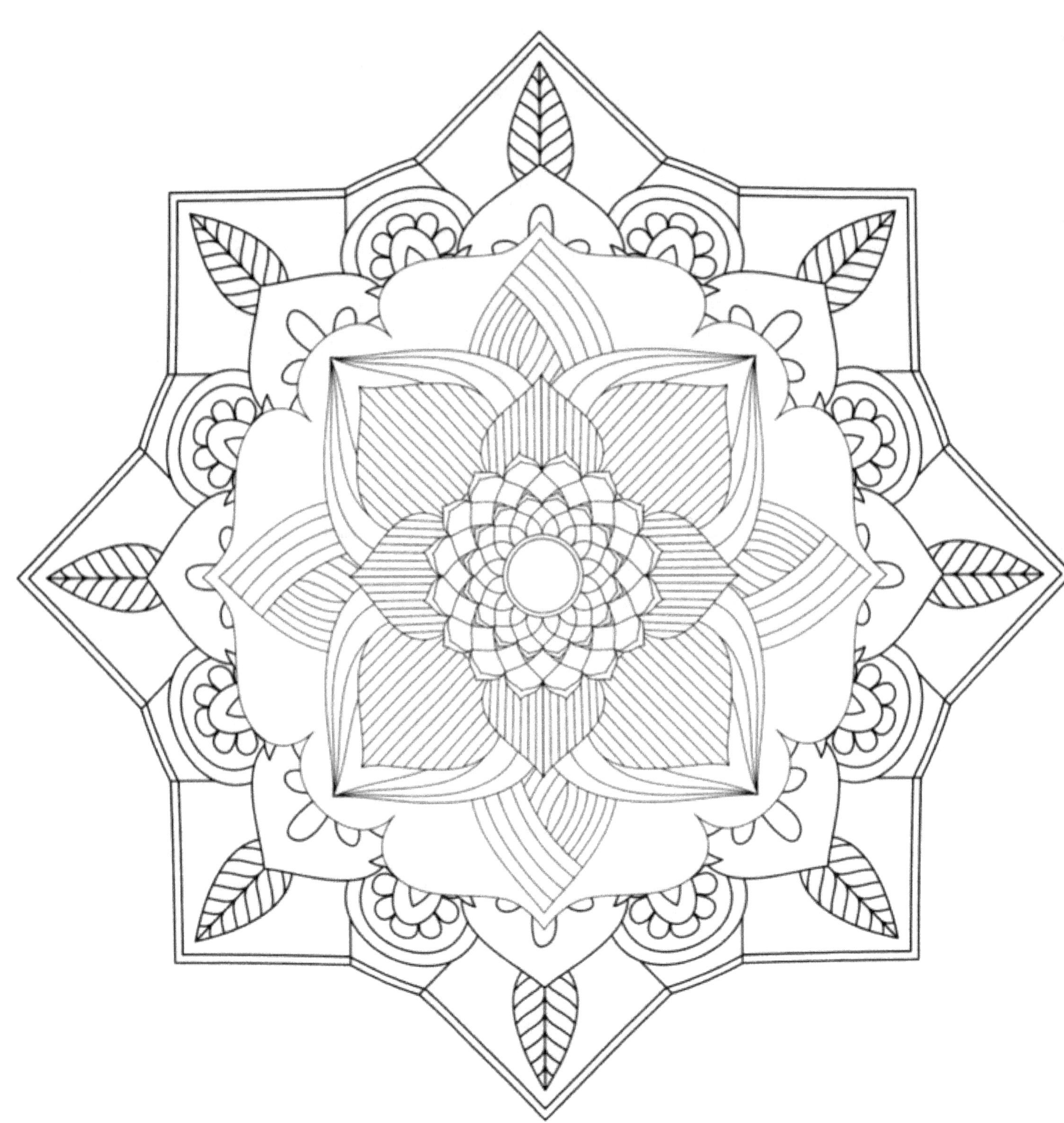

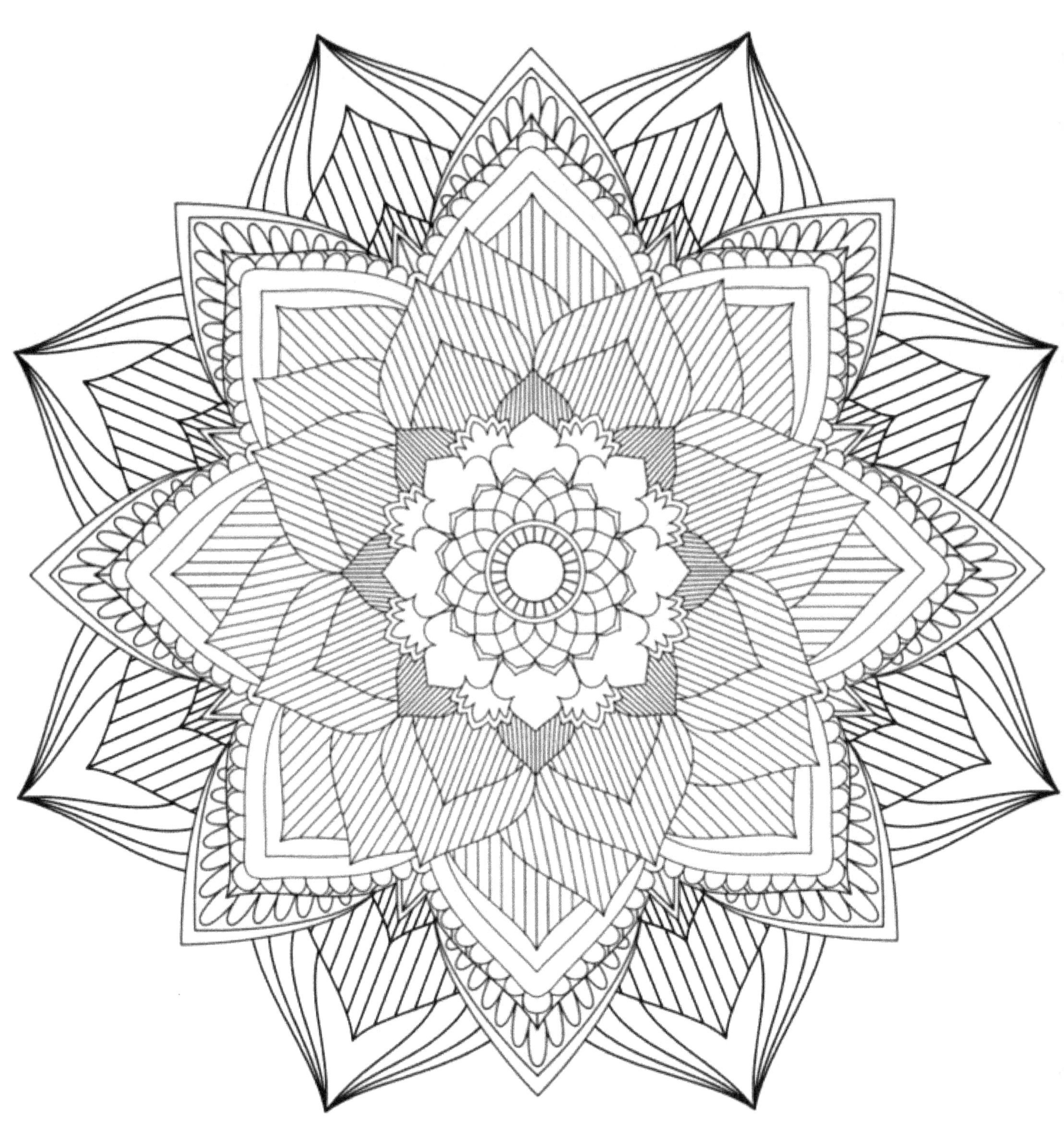

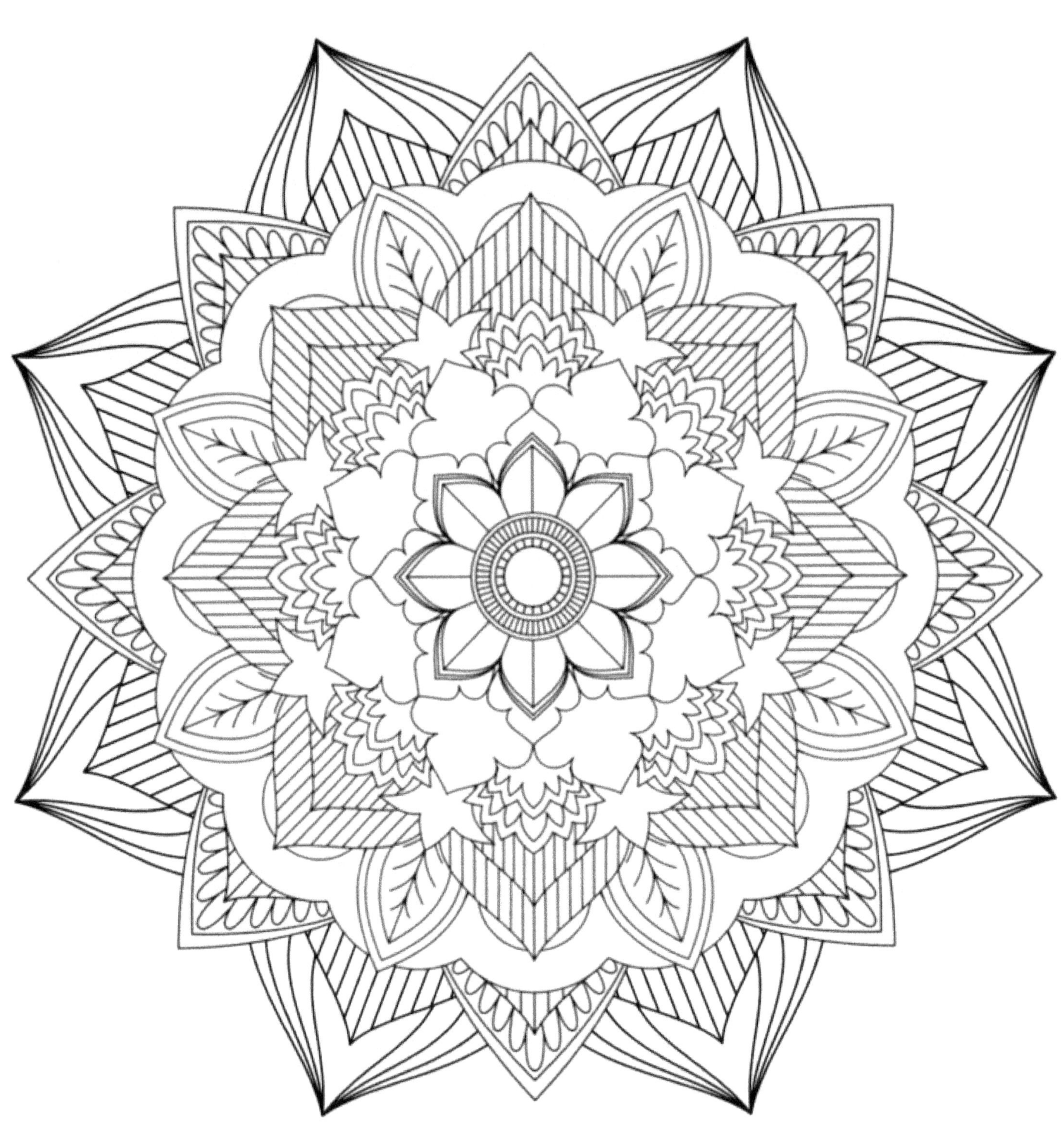

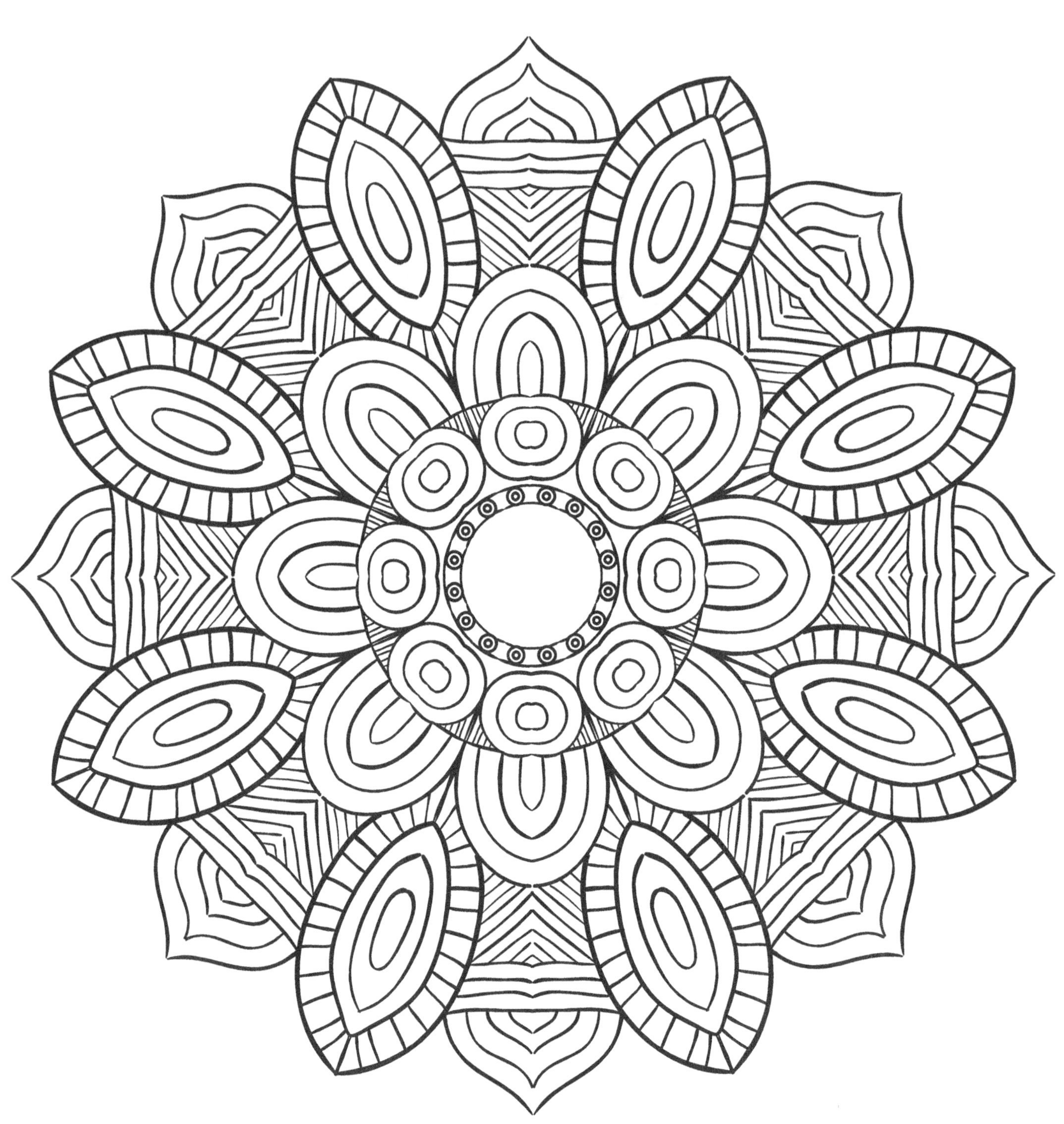

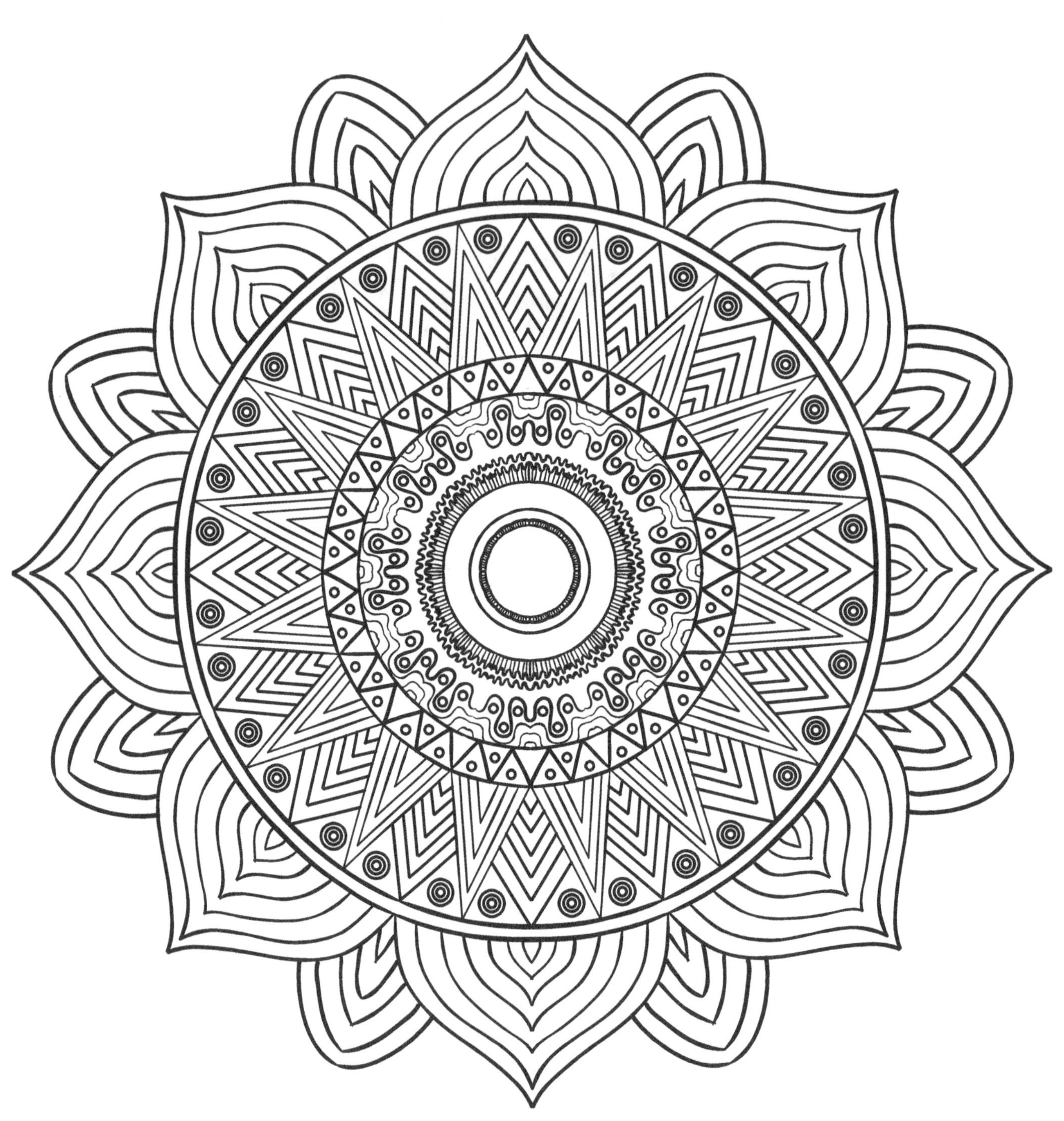

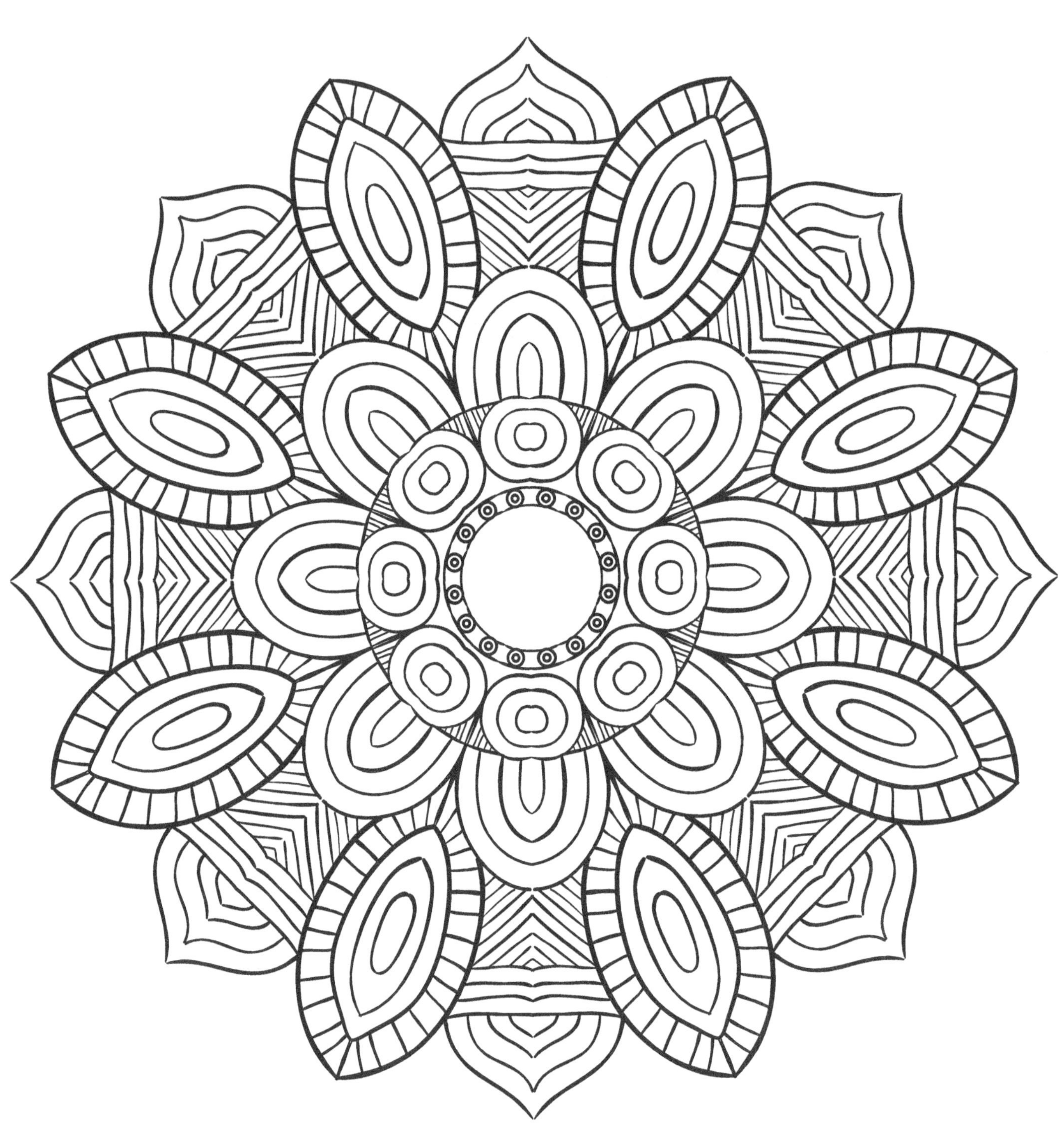

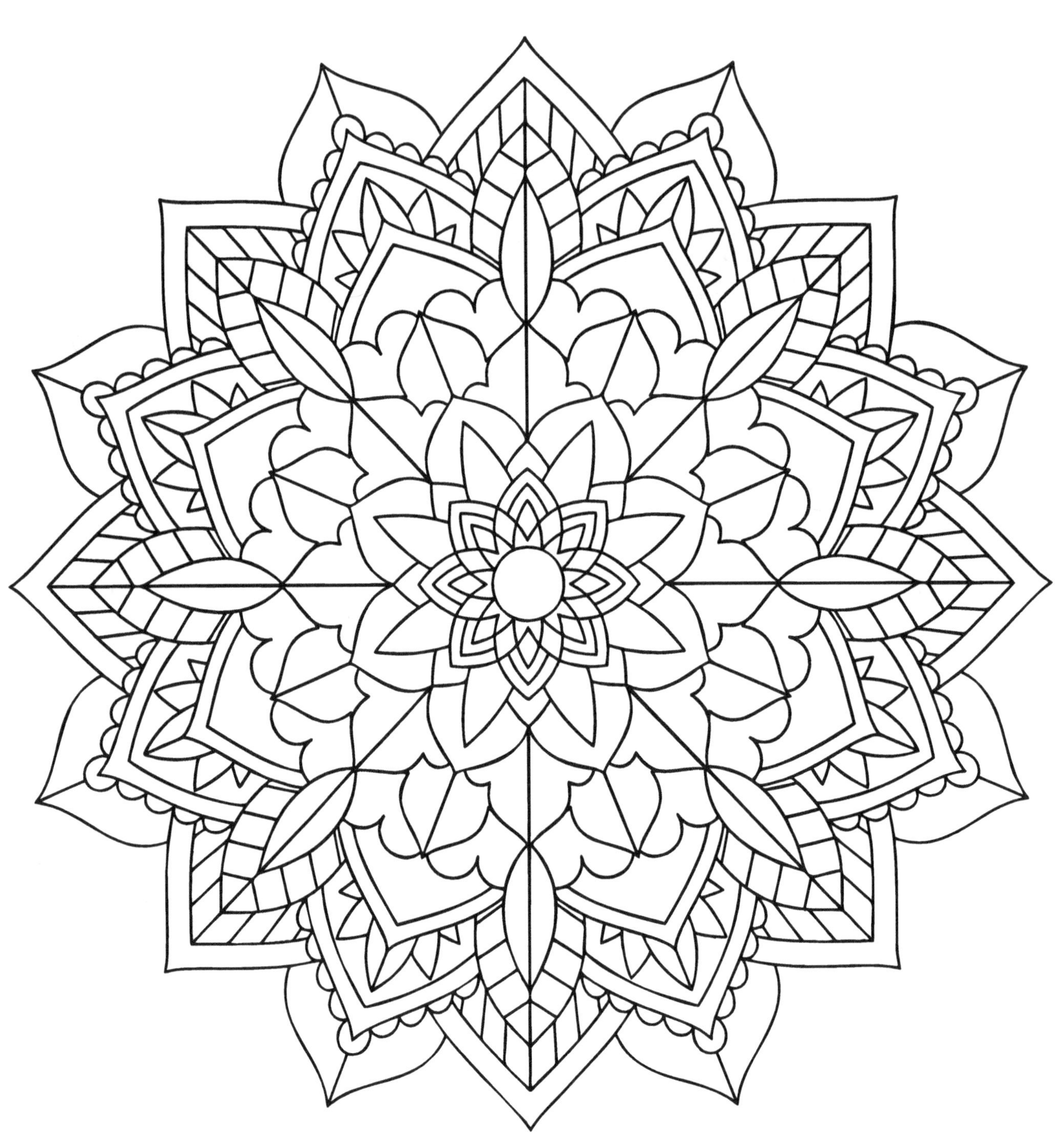

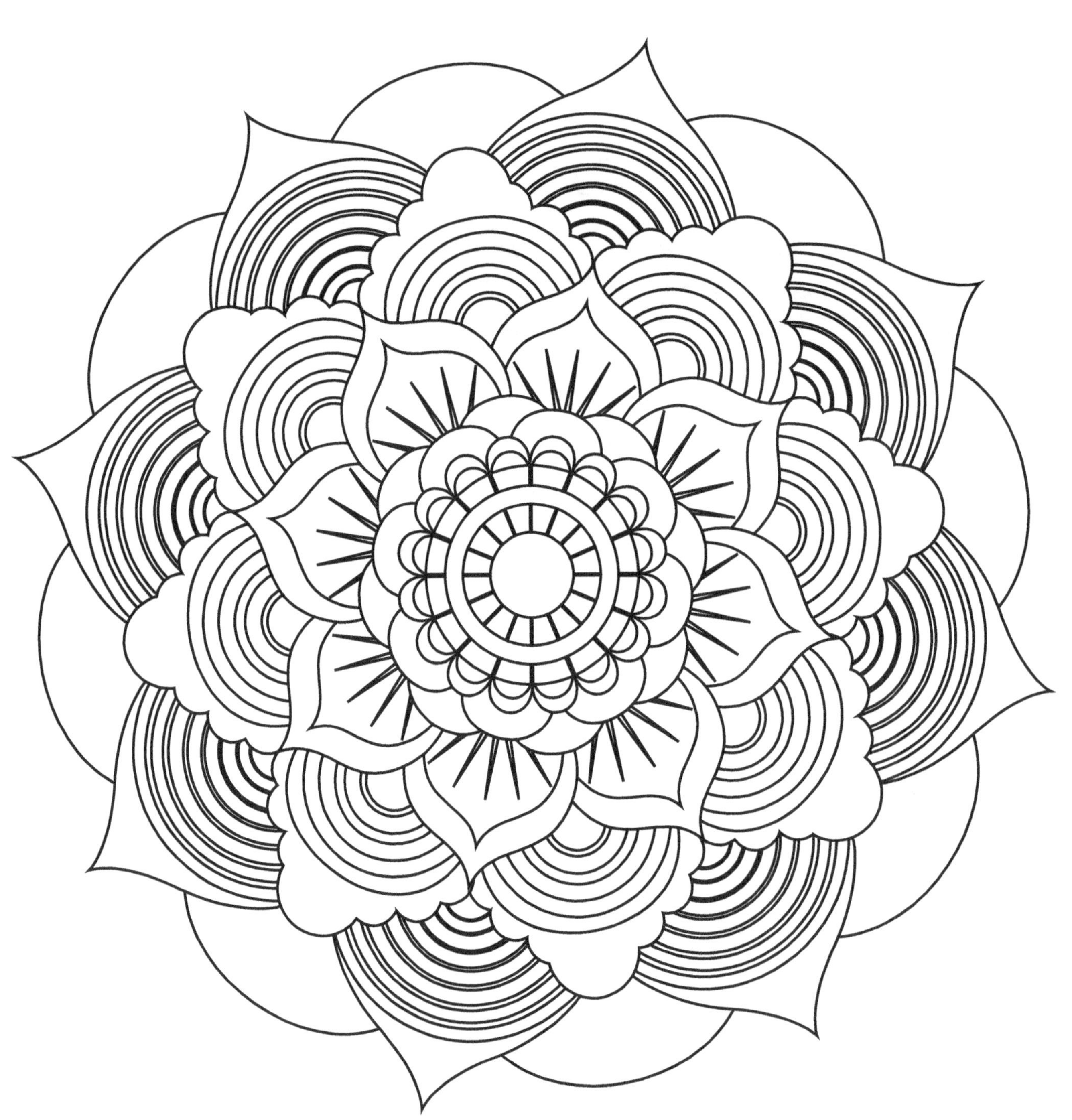